D1550843

Craven-Pamlico-Carteret
Regional Library

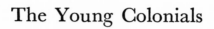

The Young Colonials

BOOKS BY ROBERT CARSE

Adult

The Age of Piracy
Blockade
Rum Row
The Moonrakers

Juvenile

The Winner
Great Venture
Winter of the Whale
Friends of the Wolf
Turnabout
Glory Haul
Hudson River Hayride
The Young Colonials

THE
YOUNG
COLONIALS

A History

By Robert Carse

Illustrated by
Gil Walker

Maps by
Bob Ritter

A W. W. NORTON BOOK

Published by

GROSSET & DUNLAP, INC.

New York

This is for
Alice and Andrew Fiske

Contents

[All maps in this book show some present-day cities and towns as well as modern state locations in order to provide familiar reference points for the reader.
Ed. note]

Acknowledgments

An expression of deep gratitude must be made here
to Mrs. S. B. Butler, Old Mystic, Conn.; and to Mrs.
Lilla Mills Hawes, of the Georgia Historical Society,
Savannah, Georgia; and to Mrs. Alvah B. Small, As-
sistant Librarian, the Maine Historical Society, Port-
land, Maine. Also to Horace P. Beck, Esq., Middle-
bury College, Middlebury, Vermont; Carl Carmer,
Esq., Irvington-on-Hudson, New York; Donald H.
Mugridge, Esq., Specialist in American History, the
Library of Congress, Washington, D.C.; Gregory F.
Price, Esq., Shelter Island, New York; and Edouard A.
Stackpole, Esq., Curator of the Marine Historical As-
sociation, Mystic Seaport, Mystic, Conn.

They have each one been of considerable help to
me in the writing of this book.

R.C.

Creek Cottage,
Shelter Island, New York,
July, 1962

"Everything was queer and surprising. It took almost two hundred years after the first landing before French explorers reached the Mississippi River, less than a third of the way across the continent. It was more than three hundred years after Columbus when the first explorers went from the Mississippi all the way across to the west coast."

——Rutherford Platt, in "Wilderness"

"Sixteen [in the colonies] is looked upon as one & twenty in England. Every Coat and Wast coat I have is so much too little for me, that it will not button within 4 inches, & I am grown tall, & tan'd with ye Sun, so yet no body guesses me to be under 20 years of age."

——Philip Thicknesse, writing home to his mother in England from Savannah, Georgia, November 3, 1763.

Preface

The settlement of the North American continent was a great, dangerous experiment that almost failed. It followed after the voyages of discovery that had begun with the Norsemen and were continued by the Portuguese, the Spanish, English, French and Dutch into the first part of the seventeenth century. There was still very little known about the New World, and never before had people gone three thousand miles across an ocean to make their homes in an absolute wilderness.

That demanded tremendous courage and daring, and in the main the settlers possessed the needed qualities or the entire idea of colonization would have eventually failed. Life was rough right from the start, and stayed so for a long time. Wild animals, wolves, panthers, lynx and bear were a threat for more than a hundred years to the inhabitants of the New England townships. The first road between Rhode Island and Connecticut was built in 1722, and most people insisted yet that it was easier, if not safer, to travel by sea. When Thomas Jefferson was in his early teens in the 1750's wolf bounties were being paid in his home county of Albemarle in Virginia. The pelt of a young wolf brought seventy pounds of tobacco, and a big one twice as much.

The Spanish had been, of course, the first to settle in the New World and on the Caribbean islands. The Dutch, great traders and sailors, soon came after them, and then the French. But the colonists of these three nations were really content to live by trade and barter with the Indians, and in the case of the Spanish, what they could loot in the way of precious metal. It was the English who were driven by land hunger, who sought to clear the forest to create "plantations" and farms.

Most of the Englishmen came out with the deep, passionate desire to make a new career, find a home for their wives and children. They had been denied the chance in seventeenth century England. Sheep farming had taken over a lot of the available land. Open fields and commons had been converted into pastures and grazing areas. A man had a hard time to hold land as a tenant farmer.

So by the hundreds, and afterwards the thousands, they came out in the wet discomfort, the gloom and stink of the ships' holds to the New World. They were joined by all sorts of people whom the King or his officials no longer wanted at home. These were political offenders, felons, indentured people, children or adults who had been "trepanned," knocked over the head and stolen off the streets of seaport towns, sold to a corrupt shipmaster for a few pounds; and soldiers and sailors who now in the years of peace were restive, unemployed, and looked forward to adventure, excitement and possibly a life of piracy.

The effect of English expansion overseas was explosive. There had been at the time of the signing of the peace with Spain in 1604 no English colonies anywhere. But by the end of the century twenty of them were along the Atlantic Coast and in the Caribbean. Those colonies contained nearly two hundred and twenty-five thousand people, most of whom were of English stock. They had conquered the sea, the forest and the jungle, Indians and wild beasts. They were in the New World to stay. The story of how they established themselves on the frontier is like none other in history.

It was in the main an achievement of individuals, or families, a small, isolated group sometimes hundreds of miles away from the nearest neighbor. The close-knit life that had existed in England was denied by the sheer vastness of this continent. Some signs of it clung still in Boston and New York and Philadelphia as they grew from towns into cities. But on the frontier, and even on the edges of the bigger towns, self-reliance was necessary for survival.

The companies of merchant adventurers or the religious sects that had sent out the original groups were principally concerned with their own interests. The colonists were all but forgotten at home, remembered only when loan payments were due, or another shipload of felons and paupers had been collected, or the Quakers had spoken too firmly in public.

Along the coast of the New World, from the wide, flat tobacco fields of tidewater Virginia to the great granite escarpments of the Maine headlands where fishermen had set up their drying racks, man was confronted by constant struggle. For over two hundred years, in any of the mainland colonies, Indians were to be feared, expected to maraud, attack. Wolves made nightly raids on cattle pens and barns, would snatch a small child or even the family dog during daylight if the settler and his wife were not watchful. Fierce, huge, bald eagles swept lambs from off the Maine island pastures while the farmers stood foolish and fired their flintlocks at a swiftly disappearing target.

Life had never been so difficult for these people, nor so dangerous, and yet most of them survived, and many flourished. George Washington completed his education fighting Indians before he became a planter. Thomas Jefferson when he went to college in Williamsburg left frontier conditions behind him although his people were prosperous landowners and were supposed to live in "settled" country. A famous family story was already being told about him and his encounter at the age of ten with a turkey.

His father, Colonel Peter Jefferson, had given him a gun and sent him out in the forest alone to hunt. He wanted freckled, red-haired Thomas to learn self-reliance. But Thomas had small luck. The game heard him coming, and evaded him until he came upon a turkey kept in a pen. The rest, for him, was simple. He took the turkey from the pen, fastened it to a tree with his garter and shot it. Then he went home in triumph.

The same sort of ability for quick wit and action was shown by Benjamin Franklin, the only one among the foremost leaders of the American Revolution to be brought up in a town. Franklin had been apprenticed as a printer's devil to his older brother, James, in Boston. But James had got himself into trouble with the authorities, and by September, 1723, it was Benjamin's decision that he start out on his own. While his brother had been in jail, Benjamin had run James's paper, the *New England Courant,* despite the fact he was only seventeen and had no formal education. Now, free from jail, James was jealous of what had been done with the paper. So, without much money and nothing like a recommendation, Benjamin headed for New York.

He arrived by sloop from Boston and soon discovered New York did not need any printer's apprentices. His money was just about gone, but he boarded another sloop that would take him across New York Bay to Perth Amboy in New Jersey. He planned to go on to Philadelphia and try for work there.

A squall hit the craft while she was part way to the New Jersey shore. Benjamin wrote in his autobiography:

"We met with a squall that tore our rotten sails to pieces, prevented our getting into the kill, and drove us upon Long Island. In our way a drunken Dutchman, who was a passenger, too, fell overboard; when he was sinking, I reached through the water to his shock pate and drew him up so that we got him in again."

Benjamin, the pilot and the Dutchman rode out the night at the anchor in the sloop, and the next day he reached New Jersey and began to hike for Philadelphia. He finally reached it after he had taken passage in another boat on the Delaware and rowed most of a night and a day to get to the city. But he soon found work, although he says in his autobiography, "I was very hungry, and my whole stock of cash consisted of a Dutch dollar and about a shilling in copper coin, which I gave to the boatmen for my passage."

Benjamin Franklin had a highly specialized trade which he had learned from his brother, trained in England. He was one of a very few to be so occupied. Youths and men in general throughout the colonies were being forced to give up the English style of guild work. It was no longer either practical or possible to make a living by being simply a weaver, a tanner, a cobbler, a farmer, a sailor. Once more, a whole new concept of life and work was demanded, tried, and proved to be successful.

The American frontier settler in the years before the Revolution became a real Jack-of-all-trades, and his sons along with him, and his wife and daughters became Jills, and equally as skilled in their way. On the frontier, you did everything yourself. If by bad luck or clumsiness a musket lock was broken, or a pair of shears or a scythe blade, you did without, and waited for the customary annual trip to town which took days of travel.

A man kept in his house a shoemaker's kit and leather, and a mortar and pestle, and a shelf filled with apothecary stuff, and lamps and candle and bullet molds, a supply of lead and powder, guns, pistols, a bayonet or a cutlass, and harness, and a cider press and a butter churn, a spinning wheel, and pots, pans, stone crocks, jugs and bottles, and all the fireplace equipment for cooking and baking.

The barn held axes and saws and adzes, mauls, scythes,

sickles, a hayrake, a plow, a harrow, and ox chains and chain traces for the horse, sieves, and augers, spades, picks, shovels, crowbars. There might well be a corner reserved for coopering work, tanning of leather, pickling and salting. If the family lived along water, and in the early years of bad roads most families did, there were also buoys and blocks and oars, boat-hooks, lobster spears, fish poles and creels and line, a spare anchor and cable and canvas.

The whole family worked. The women and the girls made linen shirts and tow-cloth shirts and britches, and woolen stockings and shawls and sweaters. The boys fashioned hats out of sealskin taken from the animals killed each spring offshore, or from gray squirrels, raccoons and foxes. Buckskin and lambskin were used, too, for various purposes, and cowhide for the shoes and boots which most boys hated because of their poor fit, and instead went barefoot right up until very cold weather.

But all of this family activity could not have succeeded without the constant participation of the young. Boys helped their fathers in the fields or on the water just as soon as they owned the strength. Girls worked inside with their mothers, swept, sanded the puncheon floor in the "great room" which was often combination kitchen, dining, living and bed room, took care of their younger brothers and sisters who were at the crawl and topple stage, cooked, sewed, fed the chickens and the stock.

There was great incentive for young people to work hard. Couples married early on the frontier, girls sometimes at fourteen, boys around sixteen. They were usually given a piece of land near the homes of their parents, and started out with a cow, a couple of chickens and whatever furniture could be spared or was made by the groom in his free time before marriage.

Boys who lived on the coast often went to sea by the age of ten. It was common habit in Maine for a man to "swing off" in the fall in a ketch loaded with salt cod and lumber for the West Indies. He would take a boy or two along to lend a hand. They rode the northwesterlies on down to the islands, bartered their cargo for sugar, rum and tobacco, waited to catch the southwesterlies in the spring, and got back home in time for late planting.

A boy's shares after several lucky voyages might be enough for him to buy a sturdy lateen-rigged ketch of about thirty tons. He could take her almost anywhere, and trade from Maine on down past Massachusetts to New York, the Delaware and Chesapeake settlements, the Caribbean islands and then Europe. When he was eighteen or twenty, he was a highly skilled shipmaster, and knew the ways, the trade practices and principal ports of half a dozen countries.

The first New England fortunes were made by shipmasters engaged in overseas trade. They were the men who when the Revolution came took the new, small navy to sea and fought the King's ships and a number of times defeated them. Their stay-ashore brothers and the men brought up inland went with Washington on the long, weary and bloody road that ended at Yorktown.

Enormous persistence was needed for that. A stubborn, almost incredible kind of courage was asked to get to

Yorktown. Still, during all the years of colonial life, the American people had taught themselves how to meet danger, and finally find some way to conquer it.

In this book are the stories of seven young people of the colonies. John Milledge was the head of his family before he was twelve; John Gyles hated and fought Indians with good reason and much success at fourteen; seven-year-old Eunice Williams survived a 300-mile winter march as a captive of Indians and later found an unusual destiny among them; John Scott, driven out of England as a political criminal at age eleven, fought against overwhelming forces of prejudice and injustice; so in her way did gently bred Anna Green Winslow fight an equally relentless enemy which ultimately took her life; David Gardiner risked his life for the island which even today bears his name and is owned by his descendants; Henry Spelman, son of an Oxford don, stowed away to America where he became one of our first Indian scouts and frontiersmen at the age of thirteen.

All were different and yet all somehow found early in life the same inner strength that made the dangerous experiment a success.

R. C.

The Young Colonials

THERE WAS never any doubt that Henry Spelman was a runaway, and skipped out from home on his own. The idea always pleased him, and he thoroughly believed it. A considerable amount of truth was of course shown by the fact that he did leave Oxford without his father's permission, and for a son of a knight and Oxford don to stow away aboard a Virginia-bound ship was quite unusual. He might readily also have been in some sort of momentary trouble.

Still, behind his action were many forces that sent him. Henry would have been a Crusader in another age, or gone to Cathay with Marco Polo. For him, in his time, he was drawn inevitably to the New World.

These were the great years for England, and were to make what was known later as the Golden Age. The armada of 130 ships sent by Philip II of Spain had been smashed by English gunners and violent storms in 1588, and the little island nation was suddenly a world power. Under orders from Queen Elizabeth, the famous captains, Raleigh, Drake, Hawkins, Frobisher and

Davys, went back to their work of exploration and the seizure of what should belong to England in the New World.

Henry was a very small boy in 1603 when Queen Elizabeth died. Her influence strongly persisted, though, in all English thinking, and at Oxford there had gathered an extremely capable group of New World historians and cartographers. Henry's father was a member of it and the leader, Richard Hakluyt, was an Oxford graduate. His main study was "Principall Navigations, Voiages, and Discoveries of the English Nation."

Henry knew Dr. Hakluyt. There must have been many evenings when he and his brothers sat silent while the firelight wavered over the panelled walls of their father's library and the hunched little doctor talked and talked and talked about the New World.

When Henry chose to run away, he left very well-informed.

Chapter I

THE FIRST
INDIAN SCOUT

Henry Spelman of Oxford, England, was very probably
the first real frontiersman in the American colonies,
and certainly there was nobody younger. Henry
stowed away on a ship bound for Virginia when he
was twelve, and a few months later he was living with
an Indian chief in the primeval forest of the upper
Potomac River country.

It is not exactly clear just why Henry left home in
1609. His father was Sir Henry Spelman, an historian,
antiquarian and scholar at Oxford University. Henry
was his third son, and must have shared with his
brothers and the rest of the family a quite pleasant
home life. But several years after his arrival in Virginia, when he had the time and could find pen and
paper, he wrote a partial explanation. "Being in dis-
pleasure of my frendes and desirous to see other coun-

treyes," he left, and with no intention to return.

A boy who came from a family as well-known as his could not get out of a town like Oxford in daylight and miss being recognized. That would mean that after only a couple of hours head start Sir Henry would organize a search. Young Henry, brought back by the bailiffs, would be very thoroughly whipped, and confined, and closely watched. So Henry must have hidden away somewhere in one of the college quadrangles, or possibly under a deep archway of Magdalen Tower, right on High Street. Then, while the bells of the many churches in the ancient town began to ring evensong, he slid out and loped through the lengthening shadows along High Street.

From it, he turned off into a maze of alleys and mews and closes that led him to the Meadows. He was too smart to take Folly Bridge over the Isis River, or get too close too soon to any frequently used road. Here in the open spaces of the Meadows he felt fully safe, and among the willows, past the famous swimming hole that was called Parson's Pleasure, he had quite likely secured a punt to take him across the Cherwell. When he was on the other side of the river, he could hide for as long as he wished on Marston Moor, or head straight on for London, swing off to Plymouth and the West country.

But he could not help his heart pounding hard when he jumped from the punt on the far side of the Cherwell. Bats had begun to blunder around his head in the last of the dusk. The usual night fog of the Thames River valley was setting in, and he could hardly see the square-built Norman tower of Oxford Castle, or Christ Church, or Magdalen. He was twelve years old, and very hungry, suddenly very alone. He could still get in the punt, pole across and soon be home.

Henry Spelman turned, and went on over Marston Moor. He jogged throughout the night along the narrow, walled lanes that took him up-hill to Elsfield. Then it was Chipping Norton, Wheatley, High Wycombe, and the main road to London. But Henry did not want London. He knew that in this month of June a flotilla was about to sail from Plymouth for Virginia.

He very probably crawled under a hedgerow along

the Plymouth road and let exhausted sleep take care of hunger for a few hours. Then he kept on at his steady jogtrot, hour after hour. But it is possible also that he had a silver piece or two, saved from his allowance, bought food at taverns, and hitched rides with wagoners and farmers on their way in carts to the market towns.

But he forgot both hunger and homesickness once he was in Plymouth. Give him a few more hours, he promised himself as he walked the quays of the famous port, and he would have a ship. His former friends back in Oxford might well be surprised. Henry Spelman was certainly on his way to the New World.

The ship he picked was named *Unity*. She lay at anchor off the Hoe, and was part of a nine ship flotilla being sent to Virginia for the relief and assistance of the settlers of the Jamestown colony. Vice Admiral Sir Christopher Newport, the founder of the colony, was in command of the flotilla, and with him were Admiral Sir George Somers and the new governor, Sir Thomas Gates. Five hundred men, women and children were aboard the ships, and a great quantity of supplies.

Conditions were extremely serious at Jamestown. Help was badly needed there. The colony, founded in May, 1607, must have supplies of food, clothing and medicine as soon as possible or the little group perched on the shore of the James River would perish.

But Henry Spelman knew nothing of this before the flotilla sailed. He must have sneaked aboard *Unity* from a cargo lighter, and then was kept occupied staying out of the way of the bosun and the officers of the ship. He peered anxiously over the bulwark at the Hoe and sighed with relief as sail canvas was spread and the high-hulled ship swung out of Cawsand Bay and took her departure from Eddystone. He then drew another deep breath and approached the bosun.

He never recorded the incident, and yet the bosun must have been a very surprised if not highly perplexed man. Henry still looked like the son of a knight and an Oxford scholar, not like a quay-side waif who would stow away for reasons of sheer desperation.

Still, the bosun found work for Henry, saw that he performed it before he was fed and given a pair of sailor's canvas pants and a rope yarn for a belt.

Henry came to love *Unity*. He worked hard in her and learned his duty from the bosun and the carpenter and the other petty officers, was very pleased that he had when the ship was caught in a hurricane off Bermuda. She and the rest of the ships of the flotilla were blown far from their true courses by the vast force of the storm. For thirty-four straight hours, they were battered by the seas and the wind.

The pinnace named *Catch*, under the command of Captain Matthew Fitch, was lost with all hands. Admiral Sir George Somers's ship, *Sea-Venture*, failed to answer at all to her helm and was pitched up on a sharp coral reef at Bermuda. Her bottom planks were ripped out of her; she wallowed, crashed, settled and became almost a total wreck. Henry went thumping past her in *Unity*, his ship perilously over on her beam-ends, anything loose on deck gone long ago over the side, her sails ragged, her rigging ripped, the topmasts snapped from her at the cross-trees. She drifted more than sailed, the preposterous, lofty aftercastle acting as a lever that hurled her stubbornly broadside.

Then, even before Captain Wood, the master of *Unity*, seemed aware of it, the wind was gone. The high seas lasted hours more, though, while the sailors renewed the rigging, went aloft on the yards and set spare sails. *Unity* squared away to her course and ran alone for the Virginia coast. Mast-head lookouts gave the shout, "Land, land-ho, sir!" Captain Wood called back, "Where away?" from the quarter-deck and lifted his long-glass. Henry, down in the waist of the ship, took a toe-hold on the bulwark, lifted himself and stared. The land was a thin snuff-brown line along the horizon. "Yon's the capes and the Chesapeake," a sailor said as he passed Henry.

Jamestown was about forty miles in from the sea, Henry reckoned from what he heard from the crew. But a bosun's mate stopped his sightseeing, and he was

busy collecting dunnage and stowing hatch tarpaulins
until *Unity* rounded up in six fathoms of water and
let the anchor go off the settlement. Henry took a
good look at it, and what he saw frightened him almost as much as the hurricane.

Jamestown was a collection of sagging, lopsided
huts inside a stockade whose logs had begun to
tumble apart. It stunk in the malarial summer sun; it
had the rotten-sweet stench of fever and decay and
death. The men who came down from it and met the
pinnace sent by *Unity* were stooped and yellow-faced,
and some wept, and others could only walk when they
were aided. Henry had the instant, uncontrollable
desire to be back in Oxford, no matter what his former

friends had done to him, or how strict his father was.

But then among the men who boarded *Unity* from the settlement Henry saw one who gave him hope. He was a short and sturdy man with a great, fierce beard and mustache. He strutted along the deck in fine cordovan knee-boots, and not like those of the other colonists, his corselet was polished until it shone, and his sword scabbard was very bright.

"Captain John Smith," Henry heard men around him say. "President of the council, and the best soldier they have alive in the pest-hole place."

The men kept on talking, some of them crew members, others from the Jamestown lot. The Jamestown men were weak with hunger; the food supply was nearly exhausted ashore, and lately they had been eating snakes to stay alive. Henry winced a bit and moved closer so that he could hear more. Hundreds of people had died, and less than a hundred of the original number were left. Indian raids had done it, and fever and disease, and hunger.

Henry Spelman waited patiently until he had the chance to talk with Captain John Smith. There is no record left of what was said between them. But the gently reared Oxford boy and the tough professional soldier became immediate friends, and remained so for life. John Smith took Henry ashore. He made him his personal charge, and some weeks later conducted him up-river aboard ship to meet and stay with Indians.

Henry had absolutely no liking for Jamestown, and never changed his mind about it. It was to him a pest-hole, a trap. The people who lived there were tragically dependent on England; they lived in England in their minds. If they did not get supplies from the home country, they would die. They were afraid of the Indians, afraid of the forest, and of the whole continent.

So they scrabbled in their little gardens inside the tumble-down stockade, or they sat dully waiting to die in front of their huts. None of them except Captain Smith and a few more hardy men had ventured inland from the stockade. The usual excuse for the others was that a matchlock gun had a range of no more than fifty yards, and some of the guns weighed as much as fifty pounds, would not fire in wet weather, were small help in the forest against either game or Indians. But the Indians, of course, could make their arrows kill up to a range of forty yards. The settlers sat on the heels of their rotting boots in the stockade and swatted at mosquitoes, shuddered with malaria pangs, and wondered, more and more vaguely, why they had ever left home.

Captain John Smith had been captured with a pair of companions when hunting in January, 1607 in the Chickahominy swamp. Two hundred braves under the command of a famous chieftain, Opechancanough, encircled and then ambushed them. Smith's companions were killed in the melee. Smith killed two warriors, grasped a third to use as a shield while he retreated towards the river and his canoe. But he slipped in the swamp mire, and the brave, a young, vigorous man, got away from him, and Smith was captured.

The Indians, members of the Potomac tribe, recognized Smith as a superb soldier. His clothing was riddled with spear thrusts and arrows. Still, he stood unwounded, and over there among the bushes were the two warriors he had taken as a price for his dead companions. Opechancanough decided the Englishman should die at the stake in the village of his brother, the great, ruling chieftain of thirty tribes, Powhatan. Powhatan's home village was a pleasant place on a hill above the smooth-flowing James River. The name for it was Weromoromoco, and from it his power extended three hundred miles South and two hundred miles inland over eight thousand Indians of Algonkian stock. Smith was brought there for the awful form of Indian torture and execution, and was only saved by the quick and daring action of Pocahontas.

The story that had been so often repeated about the young Indian girl was completely true, Henry Spelman found. He was to live soon himself in the same village with Pocahontas and in his turn have his life saved by her. But one of the first things he learned about her was that her real name was not Pocahontas. That meant, in Algonkian, "tomboy," and had been given her by John Smith. Her correct name was Matoaka.

Captain Smith told Henry of Pocahontas and Powhatan as the English ship proceeded slowly up the placid reaches of the river. He planned to barter with the Indians for corn for the starving colony, and meantime he delighted in talking to this alert boy in the tar-splotched sailor pants. The Jamestown colonists were also confused about Powhatan, their powerful neighbor, Smith said. Powhatan's real name was Wahunsunakok, and Powhatan was a term of respect that in Algonkian meant "Great Chief." There was some reason for it, though, Smith admitted, because the Indians themselves often called the chieftain by his title instead of his given name.

Henry Spelman wanted to know the details about the girl, the tomboy called Pocahontas. And just how was it that Captain Smith stood here very alive, spike mustache, beard and all, on the deck of the ship when he had been taken to Powhatan's village to be executed? Maybe the girl was some kind of a witch, who could cast a spell that took Captain Smith off safe.

The captain must have smiled at Henry's naive belief in witchcraft. There were no witches along the James River, he said. None at least that he had ever met. Pocahontas had saved his life for the quite logical reason that she considered him to be her very good friend. They had come to know each other in the forest near her village while he was on hunting expeditions. He had made her toys of coral and pieces of curiously formed woods, given her the tomboy nickname after he learned from her how to speak Algonkian.

She had saved his life twice before when warriors of her tribe threatened Smith. Each time she had appealed to Powhatan, claiming her right as his daughter and a member of the tribe. The third time, Smith said, the chieftain had been a little slow to grant her wish, although he refused to have Smith tortured or burned at the stake.

Smith, bound and hurled prone, lay with his head between two boulders below the log platform on which Powhatan stood in the middle of the Indian village. A pair of stalwart and eager warriors flanked Smith and held their thick-knobbed war clubs lifted. They took practice swings at Smith's skull while Powhatan deliberated.

Henry Spelman listened with his eyes wide. He gazed ashore at the vast, unbroken ranks of the forest. He suspected any instant to hear a war-whoop, see a Potomac brave leap from behind a tree, deliver an arrow whanging at the enemy ship. This river was not like the Isis, he told himself, or the Cherwell, or the Thames. The closest he had ever come to anything that resembled life out here was to catch with his friends an occasional beaver along the banks of the Cherwell, and to take an amazed look at the wild boar which briefly showed themselves at the edges of the Headington and Bagley woods.

Henry must have asked right about then if the captain was on his way to meet with Powhatan. The answer was that Smith intended to make barter with a lesser chieftain, a man named Tanx. It is quite probable that Henry could not hide his disappointment. For when the ship anchored off Tanx's village, Captain Smith took the boy ashore with him.

They went in the ship's pinnace, the men with their weapons ready against surprise attack. Cutlasses and pistols were in their belts, and matchlocks with matches lit propped beside the thwarts. Canoes came from the beach below the village to circle around them. Henry was a bit frightened, and greatly fascinated.

The braves who handled the canoes were nearly naked in the warm summer sunshine. They wore buckskin breechclouts and moccasins; a few had necklaces of animal claws; and Tanx sported a belt of wampum, copper bands on his biceps, and eagle feathers in his hair. The braves were magnificent men, their chests deep, their arm and leg muscles smoothly compact, and when they lined up on the beach with the pinnace crew, Henry saw that they stood a good head or so taller than Captain Smith and most of the other Englishmen.

Henry was presented to Tanx, and bowed in the fashion taught him at Oxford. The braves remained grave-faced, but Captain Smith smiled a little, and complimented Henry on his manners. But Henry was already lost in study of the Indians: the skulls bared for all except the bushy scalp locks; the face paint, yellow and white, around the eyes, alongside the mouths and on the brows; the war clubs, the tomahawks with their cruel deerhorn blades; the bows, arrows and quivers; the canoes made both from bark and fire-hollowed logs. This was surely the New World, and more fantastic than his dreams. Here the warriors lived just as dangerously as the old Greeks in his father's history books.

Captain Smith must have made an arrangement with Tanx soon after he and the chieftain exchanged gifts and promises of friendship. Tanx led Henry up to the village and in sign talk explained the habits of the people to him while the squaws and the old men stared, the children moved close and fingered the ma-

terial of Henry's smock, and the dogs, really half-tamed wolves, sniffed and roughly barked. Henry was so excited for a time that he did not recognize he was alone with the Indians. Then, looking down at the beach, he saw that the pinnace was gone, and that the ship had been moved much further out into the river.

He understood that Captain Smith was playing some sort of a joke on him, also testing his courage, his ability to get along with the Indians. It was hard for him to hide his feelings of concern from the sharp-eyed Indians, but he succeeded, and settled down among them for a stay. Smith, he told himself, most probably had sailed in the pinnace further up the river to barter for corn with other Potomac clans. He and the captain were already such good friends, he was certain that Smith would come back for him.

Tanx led the stocky, fair-skinned boy along the village street between what were known as the "long houses" to the English. These were long and narrow structures built of saplings covered and roofed with bark. A passageway ran the full length at one side of each house, and in that were the fire pits for cooking and for heat in the wintertime. Buckskins hung from poles formed the inside walls of the passageway. These kept separate the combination sleeping-living quarters of the four families that shared a long house. But, Tanx explained to Henry, counting on his fingers, as many as almost a hundred people could live in one of the structures.

Henry was impressed, and could only nod his head. He knew of no way to describe his home and Oxford, and tell of such things as Tom, the great bell at Christ Church, which sounded 101 booming strokes every evening exactly at ten minutes past nine and was heard all over that part of the valley. But he was hungry, and Tanx's squaw had venison ready in the fire pit, and Tanx's sons were willing to show him how to spear fish, catch soft-shell crabs and knock a squirrel off a tree limb with a blunt-tipped arrow.

Henry spent several days with the clan. The time passed fast, and he was happy with his new friends. Then homesickness overcame him. He felt the desire to be with his own kind, speak his own language again. It felt like his head would burst every time he tried to pronounce a word in Algonkian, and the Indians with their clucking, guttural talk sounded exactly like the gobbler turkeys that flapped through the forest underbrush.

He talked with Tanx by signs, indicated that he would like to rejoin the ship. Tanx understood him and accompanied him to the river bank. The ship still lay at her anchorage well offshore, her sails furled,

her flags and pennants slack in the afternoon calm. The
chieftain knelt, and Henry wrote later about the scene
that Tanx "clapt his hand on the ground in token he
would stay there till I returned."

Henry gave a strong shout to the anchor watch
aboard the ship. Some of the men came off for him in a
boat. He nodded politely to Tanx, expressed his gratitude, jumped into the boat and asked to be rowed to
the ship. The coxswain of the boat crew headed for the
ship at once, and then confirmed what Henry had
suspected. Captain Smith and a picked group had
gone further along up the river in the pinnace after
barter corn. They should be back tomorrow, the coxswain said, and it was time the ship sailed for Jamestown. The folks there must again be about to die of
hunger.

Captain Smith was quite dour and short-spoken
when he returned in the pinnace. For all his attempts
at barter, he had only gathered a few bushels of corn
from the Indians. The great losses of cargo from sea
damage that the flotilla had suffered in the hurricane
would now be most keenly felt, and quite possibly
bring about the abandonment of Jamestown. The
people simply did not have enough food to keep them,
and would starve if they were not supplied.

Henry Spelman was about to suggest that the Indians with whom he had stayed were able to live in pretty fair style. They had all sorts of fowl and fish, and oysters and clams and mussels and crabs and eels, venison and other game, and corn and berries, and edible roots almost like the squash eaten at home. But he thought better of that after he looked into Captain Smith's brooding face.

The captain knew a good deal about the way Indians lived. The trouble was to get the lethargic, frightened mass of the colonists out of the stockade, into the forest and down to the river, to cultivate the soil, to hunt and to fish. They had to make themselves independent, and should not count upon the barrels of salt beef and fish, bread and beer and butter from England. Without a steady source of supplies, they were useless, and hopeless.

Henry decided to keep quiet until later. He would not tell the captain that he had greatly enjoyed his visit with the Potomacs, wanted very much to go back for a really long stay.

Both he and the captain rested glum at the rail when the ship came in sight of Jamestown. The settlers were down at the water's edge, expectant and impatient. "Waiting for us to feed them," Smith murmured. "This cannot go on forever."

The supply of corn was almost finished in the space

of a few weeks, although some of the men went with Smith into the forest and hunted game. Henry accompanied them on several trips, and used a bow and a quiver full of arrows he had made in the Potomac style. This must have impressed the more observant settlers, and they called a meeting with Henry present, and another boy of about his age, Thomas Savage.

It was decided that the two boys should be sent to live with Powhatan at his home village on the James. They would really serve as hostages, and assure the Indians that the whites meant them no harm. With this relationship established, the colony should be able to trade quite steadily with the various Chesapeake tribes and clans for the much-needed supplies.

Captain Smith and tall, thoughtful John Rolfe, one of the leaders among the settlers, looked quickly at Henry, and then at the other boy. Henry was smiling with joy at the chance to live in the forest. Thomas Savage, despite his name, looked unhappy, seemed to keep from scowling only because it might be thought that he was afraid. But, Henry knew, Thomas Savage was no coward, and he liked the idea of having him along in the wilderness. Life could become pretty lonely in the Indian villages, and he and Tom could talk together in their own language, remind themselves that they were English.

Powhatan accepted them readily enough when they were brought upstream in a pinnace to his principal village. He turned them over to Pocahontas and then began to barter corn for cutlasses, hatchets and blankets. It would not be long, Henry Spelman thought, before the Indians would be asking for matchlocks, powder and ball. Captain Smith had told him privately to keep close watch on Powhatan; the captain had only distrust for the chieftain, believed he would betray the English at any time. But, Henry wondered, how much would he and Tom Savage be able to do, isolated here in the middle of this tribe, even though Pocahontas was to become their friend.

The Indian girl, slim, black-haired and very intelligent, was about a year older than Henry and Tom. She was friendly with them at once, and with the sign talk he had picked up during his stay at Tanx's village, Henry was soon able to speak to her in Algonkian. The three of them went fishing together on the James, collected berries and nuts in the fall woods, hunted small game. Henry was aware, though, that he and Tom Savage were under constant scrutiny by some of Powhatan's picked warriors. It did not matter really how friendly Pocahontas was. The fact that she was Powhatan's daughter and wore a superbly finished buckskin smock, skirt and knee-high moccasins, and

eagle feathers in the snakeskin circlet around her hair
as signs of her rank meant very little.

Henry was convinced that Powhatan was an im-
placable enemy of the English. To use a good old English phrase, Powhatan bided his time now, and waited
for the settlers to destroy themselves by disease, stu-
pidity and hunger. A few boatloads of corn, the pres-
ence of a pair of big-footed English boys in his village
would not change the final outcome. The whites had
no real hold upon the magnificent country around the
Virginia bays and rivers. Soon, quite soon, Powhatan
wished, all of them would be gone, or dead.

Henry came to realize that most bitterly the night
Pocahontas risked her life to warn him and Tom Savage. He and Tom shared the corner of a long house
compartment in the village, and Pocahontas softly
knocked on the bark wall beside Henry's sleeping
bench. A war party of Potomacs was just entering the
village, she told Henry. The braves carried as many
as thirty or forty scalps, and all had belonged to
whites, to Englishmen. Henry and Tom should go and
hide in the forest. The medicine men, at Powhatan's
order, were about to call for drumming, dancing,
great celebration.

The two boys scampered into the forest, moving
from shadow to shadow. Behind them, the celebra-

tion fire flung high flames, and in the scarlet cast of light the triumphant members of the war party danced and dangled the scalps they had taken. The screams, the shouts, the drumming and the chatter of the medicine men's rattles shattered the night until above the spot where the boys crouched birds awoke on their perches, cheeped and then fled. Owls hooted in protest. Squirrels and chipmunks hurried away into the more peaceful night. But Henry Spelman crawled back until he could see the warriors who carried the scalps, and listen to their bragging to Powhatan.

Henry was able to put the complete story together later at Jamestown. The massacre had happened about October 4, 1609. A pair of small vessels under the command of Captain West and Captain Sickelmore had been sent up the Chesapeake from Jamestown to barter for corn. Each craft carried a complement of between thirty and forty men, armed and warned that the Indians might prove treacherous. But Powhatan succeeded, through the work of sub-chiefs, in tricking Sickelmore's party into ambush in the forest past his village.

John Smith's account of it reads: "Onely Jeffrey Shortridge escaped, and Pokahantas the King's daughter saved a boy called Henry Spilman, that lived many yeeres after, by her meanes, amongst the Patawomekes."

Smith was a professional soldier, and his schooling was far behind him, and he wrote in the strangely spelled English of his time. Yet the facts are clear. The ambush, except for one man, had been perfectly executed. And "Pokahantas" saved Henry "Spilman's" life, with it that of Thomas Savage. Henry stayed for several more years among the Potomacs. First, though, he sent Thomas Savage down-river to Jamestown to warn the settlers.

His own future, and his life, he was willing to gamble right here among the Indians. It is to be believed that he got Savage into a canoe somehow, most likely with the help of Pocahontas, and out into the James and on his way to Jamestown before the exultant Potomac braves had any knowledge of the fact.

Powhatan must have come to some sort of an understanding with Henry after that. During the rest of Powhatan's lifetime, the chieftain made no attempt to kill Henry. So, about a year later, while Henry was still in Potomac tribal country, the boy was able to help the colony in a very considerable way.

The colonists had finally decided in the summer of 1610 to abandon Jamestown and go back to England. Only sixty people were left out of the more than seven hundred who had come here. The few miserable belongings the survivors owned were put aboard ship, and the last of the food supplies. The royal ensign was taken from the flagstaff halyards, a trumpet blast was given as signal, the last boat trip was made between shore and ship, and on June 17 the ship stood away towards the Atlantic.

But down the river several miles from Jamestown the ship was hailed by Captain Edward Brewster in a boat. He had been sent ahead by Lord De La Warr, he said, to tell the people of De La Warr's arrival at Point Comfort. De La Warr commanded a flotilla of ships that carried a large amount of cargo and a number of people for the relief of the colony. The settlers returned to Jamestown, a little shamefaced, but eager to sample the new food supplies, meet the new governor.

Henry Spelman was not disturbed much by any of this. It was simply his choice to remain in the wilderness; he had no desire at all to go back to England. Indians attracted to the colony by the chance for favorable barter since De La Warr's arrival told him of what went on in Jamestown. So he was not surprised when a ship worked her way upstream, a boat was sent in, and he was called by name.

The captain of the ship was Samuel Argall, a veteran master and explorer. Lord De La Warr had sent him to trade, and gather if he could enough corn for an Atlantic voyage. The account written at the time reads: "Where finding an English boy those people had preserved from the furie of Powhatan, by his acquaintance, had such good usage of those kind Salvages that they fraughted his ship with corne; wherewith he returned to James Towne: and so for England, with the Lord Governour."

This statement indicated several things. First, Henry no longer lived in the same village with Powhatan. It would have been logical for him to take up with his earliest acquaintances among the "Salvages" in Tanx's clan. Still, Powhatan when he wanted to be was all-powerful, and unless a truce existed between him and Henry, the ship would never have received her supply of corn.

Captain Argall and Lord De La Warr were lucky men. There was no ambush. The corn was put aboard ship without incident. Then Argall slipped down on the current, took as passenger the governor, and sailed for England.

Henry stayed on quite steadily in the Indian country, although as he grew into his late teens he visited a good deal at Jamestown. He left some of the very best accounts of Indian life ever written, described many phases of it in his journal. His writing style makes it impossible to reproduce his language as he put his impressions down on paper.

Here, in direct, modern language is the sense of what he wrote. He witnessed all of Indian life, experienced a great part of it, and was far more than an observer or reporter. These people of whom he wrote were his close friends; he shared their life in every way. He must have fought alongside them when they were in battle against the Iroquois.

The place where they fought was a marshy ground full of reeds. This was Potomac country, so the Iroquois were brought to it in canoes. The canoes, he explained, were a kind of boat that was made in the same shape as a hog's trough, only somewhat more hollowed out, and sharper at the ends.

Warriors scattered on each side of the battle line, some little distance from each other. Then, their bows and arrows ready, they moved softly towards their enemies, sometimes squatting down and peering through the reeds for the enemy. If a warrior was hit by an arrow, and leaped up in pain and showed himself, he did not live long. He was knocked on the head, finished with a war club blow. (Henry wrote about this: "And they that kill most of their enemies are held the chiefest men among them. . . .")

But there was no great slaughter on either side. The

invading Iroquois shot away almost all their arrows. It was the familiar battle condition of shortage of ammunition. So they retreated, went back to their hog's trough canoes, some of which were big enough to hold forty warriors, and left the marsh to the Potomacs. Henry's friends had won.

It is an interesting sidelight on such a battle that the copper which Powhatan and other senior warriors wore as arm bracelets came from the Great Lakes country. They had no contact with the region except through the Iroquois, some of whose people lived that far North. The Potomacs and the Iroquois must have traded tribe-to-tribe when not at war. All of the Potomac bracelets could not be trophies taken in combat.

Henry was curious, too, about the weapons used by his friends. They carried tomahawks with deerhorn blades cross-lashed with rawhide to handles of wood

about two inches in diameter. The tomahawks when
not in use were stuck in the back part of the buckskin
girdles the warriors wore in summer. Their knives were
made out of reed splinters sharp enough to cut joints
of meat from a deer or any beast, and fashion as
needed a warrior's moccasins, pants, smock and man-
tle.

When in battle, one kind of shield they used was
made of bark, round-shaped and with pieces of wood
in back as reinforcement. These they had been taught
to make by the Iroquois. Their own type of shield was
woven out of "silk grasse" and hemp put around a
curved structure of sticks. The surface was so tough,
Henry wrote, that no arrow could penetrate it. A warrior who carried the shield in action often slung it
from his left shoulder, so his right arm would be free
for the wielding of weapons. He crouched down as he
advanced, and could almost completely protect himself behind the shield.

But Henry was interested in matrimony and dancing and games and hunting as well as war. He wrote
about marriage that when the bride approached her
young Potomac groom in the ceremony her father or
a close friend of the family brought their hands together. Then the groom's father or a friend took a long
string of beads, and measured it to the length of his

arms. He broke it over the locked hands of the couple and gave it to "ye woman's father" or the family friend who served in her father's place. "And so with much mirth and feastinge they goe togither."

His report on dancing was brief, yet vivid. There was one brave who stood in the center of a ring of his people and played upon a pipe. (Henry most probably meant a flute.) But the same brave was in any case quite talented, for he also played a rattle. Then the others started to dance, twisting their necks and bodies in time to the music, and stamping the ground. Braves passed squaws from hand to hand around the circle, and Henry wrote that it was like "our Derbyshire Hornpipe."

His description of football along the Chesapeake is very clear. Braves played against each other with a small, leather-covered ball in an open space on a beach or in a meadow. A player dropped the ball from his hand, kicked it with the top of his foot. "He that can strike (kick) the ball the farthest," Henry wrote, "winns that they play for."

The Potomac braves did not play football in the sense of English Rugby. Only the squaws and young boys did that. The game was open, and obviously demanded a great deal of running, and passing. Goals were scored pretty much in the English style, although

Henry pointed out that the players "never fight nor pull one another doune." Henry, like many other people to come after him to the frontier, was amazed by the gentle aspects of so-called savage life.

What held his main interest, though, was the Indian style of hunting. He described in the utmost detail how as many as two and sometimes three hundred warriors would go after deer in the fall. Each brave was armed with his bow and arrows, and brandished a burning stick with which the dry lowland grass was set afire. The combination of fire and smoke flustered the deer, drove them from cover, and little by little the Indians narrowed the space around the beasts. The deer were directed whenever possible down points of land, and slaughtered there, or if they leaped into the water and swam, were killed by men who waited offshore in canoes.

Deer hide was wanted more than venison, Henry wrote, and told of how the squaws accompanied their men to do the skinning and also to set up camp for the braves each night. Warriors who hunted alone were forced to take much more care than those in the mass groups. They bathed themselves and cleansed their bodies until no human scent was left. Then they camouflaged themselves in deerskins, some with the deer heads and the antlers still attached. They moved forth into the meadows slowly, weapons hidden, and for long periods of time acted like the animals they wished to kill. They would pretend to graze, and stand still, or lick themselves in full deer fashion until they were close enough to deliver the fatal arrow.

Henry's accounts stop when he was in his middle teens. He found less and less reason to be in Jamestown, and much more reason to be away, far up the beckoning waters of the Chesapeake. His life was spent as a hunter, trader, explorer, and he was often employed as an interpreter by people in the colony. Powhatan had died in April, 1616, and his brother, Opechancanough, had succeeded him. The colonists believed they could trust the chieftain, and in 1614 the famous marriage between Pocahontas and John Rolfe had been celebrated. The colony had begun to prosper, and take on many of the stuffy habits of English life and rule.

Henry found himself in trouble with the governor, Sir George Yeardley. Another interpreter whose name was Robert Poole had accused Henry under oath of having made belittling remarks about His Excellency. When Henry came to Jamestown on August 4, 1619 he was brought up on charges before the Assembly. For whatever his private reasons were, Poole swore on the stand that Henry had told Opechancanough that within a year "there would come a Governor greater than this now in place."

Sir George Yeardley was furious. He told the members of the Assembly after Poole had finished his testimony that he wanted Henry most severely punished. The members did not share the Governor's view, and some of them could hardly keep from laughter. A mild kind of compromise was reached after some discussion, and Henry Spelman was stripped of his title of captain of the troop of militia, and "condemned to performe seven years service to the Colony in the nature of Interpreter to the Governour."

The report of the trial reads that when Henry heard the sentence he only muttered "certaine words" to himself, then left the Assembly and Jamestown. He seldom came back afterward, even to serve as interpreter.

Henry Spelman was alarmed, though, by what was happening in the colony, and did his best to warn the settlers. The early massacres and ambushes by the Indians were nearly forgotten. Now people made their homes open to Indians, let them come and go as they wished. There was talk of starting a college for Indians at Henrico. The tribes were to be educated, christianized, made to wear woolen clothing and hard leather shoes, and respect the king.

Henry while he moved on his long trading voyages along the back reaches of the Chesapeake found the stockaded Indian villages much better guarded than Jamestown itself, and the outlying settler homes were completely defenseless. He realized that Opechanca-nough was no more to be trusted than Powhatan, and during the winter of 1621–1622 there were many signs of impending attack.

The Indians struck at eight o'clock in the morning on April 1, 1622 in Jamestown, and outside. They slaughtered men, women and children with ruthless hatred. Treaty after treaty had been broken by the whites. So let them die, if they could not keep their solemn word.

Henry was not near Jamestown at the time, only returned later to talk with the few survivors. He must have felt a premonition about his own future, because he was after all an Englishman and could not fully escape the hatred given his people. But late in 1622 he accepted an offer to take a vessel laden with trade goods up the Chesapeake and into the Potomac River. Another frontier trader, Captain Henry Fleet, went with him, and a crew of twenty-six men.

Henry Spelman sailed the ship along the Potomac to an anchorage opposite the present site of Washington. The anchor was let go, and held the ground. Then he and twenty-one men, all armed, went ashore to meet with the Indians and arrange for trade. But this was territory that belonged to the Anacostan tribe. He was not as well known here as he was down-river.

The ambush was sudden, and thoroughly planned. Warriors in canoes that had been hidden in underbrush alongshore paddled swiftly out and tried to overcome the five men left aboard. They were only driven off when a sailor was able to reach a cannon, and fire the piece. The warriors dived into the river for protection and swam away to safety.

But the shore ambush was perfectly executed. The sailors left aboard heard great, abrupt yelling from the edge of the forest. There were a few shots, the sounds of blows. Then, out of the brown winter foliage, a man's head was thrust, rolled down the bank into the river. The sailors did not wait any longer. They hauled anchor and sailed for the Chesapeake and Jamestown.

Captain John Smith heard about Henry Spelman's death in England. The captain had left the colony some years ago after troubles of his own with the authorities. But he remembered Henry very well, and he wrote of him:

"Thus things proceed and vary not a jot,
"Whether we know them, or we know them not."

This not particularly profound bit of doggerel did not express anything like the tribute Henry Spelman deserved. Henry had lived for twelve long, dangerous and extraordinary years among a primitive people in wilderness, the first of his kind in America. When he died at the age of twenty-four it was great tragedy. Men who possessed his courage, his knowledge and integrity were to be needed in the colonies for many years to come.

NO OTHER record quite like the diary kept by Anna Green Winslow remains for us. Anna was in many ways an extraordinary girl, and surely a very courageous, witty and charming one. During her short life, she gave evidence of the utmost best of the colonial spirit.

She was brave in adversity and pain, and persevered with her assigned work despite nearly any obstacle. It has been said of her that she is probably the youngest diarist on record, and without doubt a journal such as she kept is very rare.

Anna shows with great accuracy, and sensitivity and humor the life of upper-class Boston in the fateful years just before the Revolution, and also how really innocent she was. As she wrote gaily to her father that she had become a "daughter of liberty" she could not have fully understood the tragedy of his situation and her own. Although born in the colonies, he was an officer in the king's service sworn to remain loyal. While the revolution surged around them, both Anna and he would learn the price of supporting the king.

63

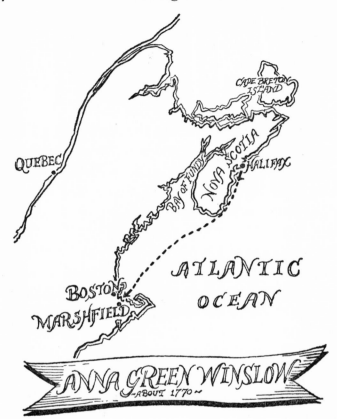

ANNA GREEN WINSLOW
~ABOUT 1770~

Chapter 2

A DAUGHTER
OF LIBERTY

Right from the moment the ship left the rough log wharf in Cumberland, Nova Scotia, and headed off-shore, Anna Green Winslow had to remind herself that she was being sent from home to become lady-like. Her mother had thoroughly warned her about the temptations of shipboard, and told her just how to act. But it was hard to be prim all the time when you were ten years old and this was 1770 and your first time away from a small town.

Anna was intensely excited. She was on her way to stay with her parents' relatives in Boston, go through there what was to her the quite mysterious, immensely complicated procedure of doing always what was "proper" and "correct." Her father was Commissary General of the British forces in Nova Scotia. Without doubt, his young daughter had been entrusted to the care of friends aboard, and that also a few words had been spoken about her to the master of the ship.

But these facts did not keep Anna from scampering around the decks of the coastwise vessel, or asking questions of the sailors, and on occasion, talking just a bit about her ancestor, Mary Chilton. She had all of Mary Chilton's story straight.

When the *Mayflower* anchored off Provincetown on Cape Cod after the long voyage in 1620, the crew were very careful. It was already late November, and some place ashore had to be found for the colony before winter. But the Massachusetts coast was an almost unknown region to the people aboard, and Indians had been seen in the bush tangle above the beaches. So great caution should be taken.

For ten days, only parties of armed men went ashore in the long-boat. Then some of the other people started ashore on their own. They could no longer just stand and stare at the new continent which was to be their home.

Mary Chilton, a "sprightly young girl" according to the account left about her, was the first of the people to reach the beach. She hitched her skirts and petticoats above her knees, and jumped from the bottom of the *Mayflower's* ladder into the water. It was shockingly cold, still she waded in through clam and mussel banks and holes between sand bars until she was on solid land.

Some of the men remonstrated with her for what they thought was her rash action. The rest of them liked her for it, and one of those was John Winslow, the brother of Edward Winslow, the Governor. Mary Chilton fell in love with John and married him soon after the colony was established at Plymouth.

Anna Green Winslow was Mary Chilton's direct descendant in the sixth generation. She had been fully instructed in family history, and know that here in Boston she would meet many relatives. Her folks were of Boston and Massachusetts Bay stock. Her father, born in Boston in 1727 and baptized at the Old South Church, was Joshua Winslow. He had been a professional soldier in the British Army most of his life, served as a lieutenant when he was eighteen in Colonel Moore's regiment and fought against the French in the capture of Louisburg.

Anna was very proud of him and his long red coat with the white silk facings, brass buttons and sword sash. She loved him dearly, although she loved her mother more. Now, with the ship entering Boston harbor and tacking on a slant of wind for Long Wharf, she keenly missed her mother. She wished her mother were here with her, and not so far away in Cumberland.

But Anna was warmly greeted when the ship tied
up at the wharf. She was met by her mother's sister,
Mrs. John Deming. There was a carriage waiting, because Anna was not really too strong, and had brought
quite a bit of luggage with her. A carriage ride over
cobble stones, after the rough country roads and
springless carts of Nova Scotia, was a thrill to Anna.
She leaned out of the window to watch the people in
the streets, stare at the shop signs, marvel at the qual-
ity of some of the women's dresses, shawls and bon-
nets, and then asked her aunt rapid-fire questions.

Anna was a thin, brown-haired girl, rather tall for
her age, with a short nose, a wide and humorous
mouth, and very bright, very intelligent eyes. Her aunt,
whom she called "Aunt Deming," liked her at once,
and called her "Nanny" when she was good, several
other things when she was bad. All in all, though, during the three years Anna spent with her aunt and uncle
in Boston she was deeply happy. She was ill a good
deal of the time, but that could not be helped, she told
herself, and with her buoyant nature she was able to
keep busy, and even gay.

The Demings lived in Central Court, off Washington
Street, almost in the center of Boston. The red brick
houses with their neat white window trim and shiny

brass door fittings appeared very formal and imposing to Anna. Then she found that her Aunt Deming had a couple of young girls in their early teens living in the house. They were boarders, girls from country families who had come to the city, much like Anna herself, to get educated and learn "manners." Anna was glad. She liked to make friends, and these seemed like nice girls.

Aunt Deming took her almost immediately to meet the rest of her Boston relatives. While they walked along the narrow, brick-paved streets, Anna skipping a bit and tempted to jump over a horse block here and there, she was told that her Uncle John Deming was an ensign in the Ancient and Honorable Company of Artillery, and very active in the affairs of the Old South Church. There was a great deal more that Anna was going to hear about the Old South Church; nearly all of her family, her future friends and acquaintances in Boston were members of it, regularly attended it.

Anna was not aware of the fact at the time, still her family belonged to the very top group of Boston society. A number of the men shared her father's Loyalist beliefs and had great respect for the King. They looked upon Boston as really an overseas outpost, a small, colonial London. They waited impatiently for the next ship from London, the latest news and gossip and fashions. Their wives and children were dressed in London styles, and Anna was surprised at the splendor of some of her cousins' costumes.

She and Aunt Deming passed several hours in a visit at her Uncle Ebenezer Storer's house on Sudbury Street. This house had been built in 1700, and was considered to be one of the most beautiful in the city. Her Uncle Ebenezer was a wealthy man, with a great liking for books and knowledge, and served for years as the treasurer of Harvard College. The house was designed on classical lines, was three stories high, had

the protection of a huge old English elm that reared up from the sidewalk in front, and an equally big sycamore out in the backyard. The rooms were long and low, and either wainscoated or panelled, and the massive furniture was made of mahogany. Glass globes that reflected everything around them were fixed to the ceiling beams, and the chimney place in the dining room was lined with ornamental Dutch tile. Upstairs was a large library, and charts of the world, and a telescope and a star-finder.

Anna was so awed she could barely drink her tea or appreciate her newly met cousins' jokes. But she came often afterwards to the Sudbury Street house. She danced many minuets on the crimson and green Persian carpet in the living room, sat with a book on the window-seat that looked out over the garden. Her Aunt Deming's house was nice enough, but it held none of the marvellous, deep comfort of this.

She must start a diary, Anna told herself when she got back home with Aunt Deming from visiting. Her mother and father, even her little brother, John Henry, still too young to read, should know what went on here in the astonishing city of Boston. Anyhow, she had promised her mother faithfully that she would write, and it was time that she got busy.

Anna took some of her allowance and bought a large notebook of ruled paper. She kept her diary in that for the years from 1771 to 1773, with only a few interruptions, and just three small ink blots. Her writing was neat and careful, each letter perfectly formed. She had great pride in keeping the diary, and told all her secret thoughts to it. By reading the seventy-two pages that it covers, a vast amount can be learned about a young girl in Boston in the crucial, tense years just before the Revolution, and how she lived and worked and played, and was able to hold hidden from herself for long periods of time the fact that she was increasingly ill.

Anna's people were Puritans, and very strict. Physical pain meant very little if anything to them. There was no excuse that they would take for what they called "slothfulness." Anna often had heavy colds, and bouts of fever that shook her thin body for hours on end. Still, she had her work to do, and she did it.

With her Aunt Deming around to superintend, Anna knitted lace and made fine network; she spun linen thread and woolen yarn. She made purses, and embroidered pocketbooks, and plaited watch strings for her uncle and her other male relatives, and learned to sew patchwork quilts. Down in the big kitchen on the ground floor of the house, she took her cooking

lessons, and was taught how to make what she spelled
as "pyes."

She went to three different schools. Sewing was
taught at one, dancing at another, and handwriting at
the third. Anna liked the dancing fine, but she knew
the importance of handwriting. That was the greatest
accomplishment anybody could have in the Boston of
her time. She worked long hours forming her letters,
and showed Aunt Deming each entry in her diary, was
severely criticized, and made to correct mistakes. Then
she had her Bible to read, and her catechisms to be
answered. There were the sermons at Old South
Church that lasted all of Sunday morning, and Thursday Lecture, and in-between spells of family Bible
reading and prayer.

But life had its brighter side, and Anna took full advantage of it. She spent many afternoons out visiting
by herself, drinking tea, gossiping, dancing or playing games at the homes of friends and relatives. Whenever she could, she visited the Storer family in Sudbury Street, borrowed one of her uncle's books and
made herself comfortable on the green damask window-seat. She had also an amazing amount of clothes
to try on, or a hat to buy with some of her allowance
from home, or a dancing party to attend.

The dancing parties, in the language of that time,

were called routs. But Anna had her own name for them. She called them "constitutions" in her diary, and she admitted that she greatly enjoyed herself. It did not seem strange to her that no boys were invited to these routs, although all their sisters and girl cousins were there. Anna just seemed to take it for granted that the Boston boys of her age group were kept apart, and were permitted to buy liquor in any dram-shop or tavern, and very likely would have refused to come to the routs even if asked.

Anna was all dressed up for one occasion, and mentioned every bit of her costume in her diary. She wrote:

"I was dress'd in my yellow coat, my black bib & apron, my pompedore shoes, the cap my aunt Storer sometime since presented me with (blue ribbins on it) & a very handsome loket in the shape of a hart she gave me—the past pin my Hon'd Papa presented me with in my cap, My new cloak & bonnett on, my pompedore gloves, &c., &c. And I would tell you that *for the first time, they all lik'd my dress very much.* My cloak and bonnett are really very handsome. . . ."

It is easy to believe that Anna was a better dancer than a speller. She meant heart when she wrote "hart," and paste when she put down "past," and her spelling of locket is pretty shaky. The "pompedore" gloves and

slippers she wore happened to be the very height of
fashion at the time, and no doubt they took their name
from the famous Marquise de Pompadour, in France.

Anna enjoyed herself tremendously at the rout held
January 17, and left a complete account of it in her
diary. Her occasional spelling mistakes can be for-
given. "Nanny" Winslow, as her friends called her,
was a fine reporter. She takes you right back to 1771

and Boston on a chill and snowy afternoon. Hundreds
of candles were already lit in the great house where
the children and their elders gathered. The grave,
pink-cheeked little girls compared each others' dresses,
and clattered upstairs. Then, as the music began, they
chose partners, curtseyed, swung out slowly upon the
polished floor and danced. Nanny Winslow wrote:

"There was a large company assembled on a handsome, large upper room in the new end of the house. We had two fiddles, & I had the honor to open the diversion of the evening in a minuet with miss Soley." When the formal numbers were finished, there was more gayety and freedom, because she wrote that they "form'd for country dancing." Soon after that refreshments were served. "Our treat was nuts, raisins, Cakes, Wine, punch, all in great plenty."

So the young teen-age girls, in their way, drank just as much as the boys. It was a period when huge quantities of alcohol were consumed, but most certainly Nanny Winslow and her friends were kept under close watch by their elders. She told her diary:

"We had a very agreeable evening from 5 to 10 o'clock. For variety we woo'd a widow, hunted the whistle, threaded the needle, & while the company was collecting (she means the adult company) we diverted ourselves with playing of pawns, no rudeness Mamma, I assure you. Aunt Deming desires you would *perticularly observe* that the eldery part of the company were *spectators only,* they mix'd not in either of the above describ'd scenes."

A good part of Nanny Winslow's life was spent at hard work, and the dancing parties were rare. She once told her diary about some of her duties:

"I hope somebody beside myself will like to eat a bit of my Boston pye, though my papa and you did not (I remember) chuse to partake of my Cumberland performance. I think I have been writing my own Praises this morning. Poor Job was forced to praise himself when no *man* would do him that justice. I am not as he was. I have made two shirts for unkle since I finished mamma's shifts."

Her mother was often in her thoughts, as the diary entries show. Still, Nanny on the arrival of a certain hat from Nova Scotia became wildly furious with Mrs. Winslow. She put down with great emphasis her feelings about it. She said:

"The black Hatt I gratefully receive as your present, but if Captain Jarvise had arrived here with it about the time he sail'd from this place for Cumberland, it would have been of more service to me, for I have been obliged to borrow."

Nanny just did not like the black hat. She was ashamed to wear it, and with it her red cloak, which she called a "Dominie." She wrote frankly:

"Now I am to leave off my black ribbins tomorrow, & am to put on my red cloak & black hatt—I hope aunt wont let me wear the black hatt with the red Dominie —for people will ask me what I have got to sell as I go along street if I do, or, how the folk at New guinee do?

"Dear mamma, you don't know the fation here—
I beg to look like other folk. You don't know what a
stir would be made in sudbury street, were I to make
my appearance there in my red Dominie & black Hatt.
But the old cloak & bonnett together will make me a
decent bonnett for common ocation. (I like that.) aunt
says, its a pitty some of the ribbins you sent won't do
for the Bonnett.—I must now close up this Journal.
With Duty, Love & Compliments as due, perticularly
to my Dear little brother (I long to see him) & Mrs.
Law, I will write to her soon.

"I am Hon'd Papa & mamma,

"Yr ever Dutiful Daughter,

"Anna Green Winslow.

"N.B. My aunt Deming dont approve of my English
& has not the fear that you will think her concern'd
in the Diction."

This was just about as close to rebellion that Nanny
ever got. Some time later, though, in May of the next
year, she objected passionately against the use of a
very fancy hair style, despite all her love of making
a fine appearance. Her objection was really because
the style would—and did—make her look ridiculous.
She told in her diary:

"Yesterday towards evening I took a walk with my

cousin Sally to see the good folks in Sudbury Street,
& found them all well. I had HEDDUS (She means
hideous) roll on. Aunt Storer said it ought to be made
less, Aunt Deming said it ought not to be made at all.
It makes my head itch, & ache, & burn like anything
Mamma. This famous roll is not made *wholly* of a red
Cow Tail, but is a mixture of that & horse hair (very
course) & a little human hair of yellow hue, that I suppose was taken out of the back part of an old wig."

Nanny had no great admiration for the local barber, a man she always referred to simply as "D—,"
and she blamed him for most of her discomfort and
humiliation. She wrote about that:

"But D— made it (our head) all carded together
and twisted up. When it first came home, aunt put it
on, & my new cap on it. She then took her apron &
measur'd me from the roots of my hair on my fore-
head to the top of my notions. I measur'd above an
inch longer than I did downwards from the roots of
my hair to the end of my chin.

"Nothing renders a young person more amiable than
virtue & modesty without the help of fals hair, red
Cow Tail, or D—. Now all this, mamma, I have just
been reading over to my aunt. She is pleas'd with my
whimsical description & grave (half grave) improve-
ment, & hopes a little fals English will not spoil the

whole with Mamma. Rome was not built in a day."

Nanny took another shot at the barber before she was through with him. She had been out visiting in her usual style, and came home to write:

"In the course of my perigrenation, as aunt calls it, I happen'd into a house where D— was attending the lady of the family. How long she was at his opperation, I know not. I saw him twist & tug & pick & cut off whole locks of gray hair at a slice. The lady telling him she would have no hair to dress next time for the space of an hour & a half. When I left them, he seeming not to be near done. This lady is not a grandmother tho' she is both old enough & gray enough to be one."

Nanny and her friends, while they visited each other's homes quite frequently and enjoyed their own private secrets and jokes, did not have many games that they played. Their lives were really quite sedate, and they were in great part miniatures of their mothers, little women. The fact that they were Puritans weighed heavily upon them, too, and only a very few holidays meant a happy time for them. Christmas was not celebrated with the joyous abandon, the fun, the gifts, the singing and dancing so popular in England. A black cloud of Puritan disapproval lay over the holiday in Massachusetts.

Nanny wrote about it very quietly:

"This day, the extremity of the cold is somewhat abated. I keept Christmas at home this year, & did a very good day's work, aunt says so. How notable I have been this week I shall tell you by & by. I spent the most part of Tuesday evening with my favorite, Miss Soley, & as she is confined by a cold & the weather still so severe that I cannot git farther, I am to visit her again before I sleep, & consult with her (or rather she with me) upon a perticular matter, which you shall know in its place. How *strangely industrious* I have been this week. I will inform you with my own hand.

"At present, I am so diligent, that I am oblig'd to use the hand & pen of my old friend, who being *near by* is better than a brother *far off*. I dont forgit dear little John Henry. So pray, mamma, don't mistake me."

For January 1, 1772 she made an entry that mentioned her only New Year's gift, a solemn and sourly expressed Puritan tract. She wrote with spirit, though, and tried to be gay:

"I wish my Papa, Mama, brother John Henry, & cousin Avery & all the rest of my acquaintance at Cumberland, Fortlaurence, Barronsfield, Greenland, Amherst, &c., a Happy New Year. I have bestow'd no new year's gift as yet. But have received one very handsome one, viz. the History of Joseph Andrews abbreviated. In nice Guilt (she means gilt) and flowers cover. This afternoon being a holiday I am going to pay my compliments in Sudbury Street."

Even St. Valentine's day was greeted without any particular elation by the Boston children of Nanny's time. She did record the observance of a strange old custom whose origin went far back into very early English history. For a woman, or a girl, the first male she saw after waking up on the holiday was supposed to be her valentine. It was Nanny's luck to look out her bedroom window and see an old, bow-legged farmer slogging along the street to market. She was quite disappointed, and spoke about him in her diary as a "plow-joger."

It might well have been that the girls of her age and her group had most of their fun while they worked. They were kept occupied a good number of hours each day. Nanny wrote in her diary about a typical winter day that she had spun thirty knots of lining yarn, partially finished a new pair of feet for the maid's stockings, read some of *Pilgrim's Progress*, then copied some text, played for a bit, put tucks in one of her uncle's shirts, and "laugh'd enough."

Later, in March, she admitted to her diary that due to sickness she had been kept home for a week. She had, though, gone to church in the carriage of a family friend, come home and begun to work. She sewed on the bosom of her uncle's shirt, mended two pairs of gloves, and mended for the wash a pair of handkerchiefs, sewed on half the border of an apron for her aunt, and ended up by reading part of the Twenty-first Chapter of Exodus and a story in a book called *The Mother's Gift.*

Then, feeling pretty self-satisfied, she wrote:

"It's now tea time. As soon as that is over, I shall spend the rest of the evening in reading to my aunt. It is near candle lighting."

Nanny Winslow kept so close to her home and her own special group, and wrote so much about them that it is a bit difficult to realize that she had other interests outside. Boston during the years she spent there was rapidly changing, and a girl as bright as she was must have sensed that. British troops were in garrison in the city, stamped the narrow streets in their thick-soled ammunition boots, were pelted by snow balls in winter, and rocks and refuse in summer. The Navigation Acts which restricted trade so heavily in favor of England and against Massachusetts were in full effect, and were violently opposed. Nanny Winslow felt proud of the boys who dared attack the garrison troops.

Many of the men who were the fathers of her young

English

friends had recently changed their political views. They were no longer Loyalist, and failed to speak up on every occasion in favor of the King and Parliament. What they wanted, they said more and more openly, was freedom from the home country. Nanny heard over, over again in the houses where she visited, "No taxation without representation."

She began to express those feelings herself. The city was filled with organizations that pledged themselves to fight for liberty. There were the Sons of Liberty, who held meetings every day and night. And there

were the Daughters of Liberty, who held spinning and
weaving bees. Nanny Winslow and her friends attended the meetings, and solemnly pledged:

"We, the daughters of those Patriots who have appeared for the public interest, do now with pleasure
engage with them in denying ourselves the drinking
of foreign tea."

Still, the King's birthday, really the biggest holiday
of the year, was celebrated with a parade on the Common and fireworks over the harbor. The Ancient and
Honorable Company of Artillery and the other militia
units turned out along with the King's troops, and
there were as yet little more than a few taunts and
bad jokes passed between colonials and regulars.
Nanny Winslow was so caught up in the political tide
that she was bewildered.

She had visited with her Aunt Deming one April
afternoon at the home of Colonel Gridley, a family
friend. The colonel had done his best with Nanny,
and explained to her about Whigs and Tories, and
what the differences were. But she could only write
down the fact in her diary, and when she wrote to her
mother and father, she completely forgot that her
father served the King as a high-ranking officer. She
may have been too eager to write about her new hat:

"I have made the purchase I told you of a few pages

agone, that is, last Thursday I purchas'd with my aunt Deming's leave, a very beautiful white feather hat, that is, the outside, which is a bit of white hollond with the feathers sew'd on it in the most curious manner, white and unsullyed as the falling snow. This hat I have long been saving my money to procure, for which I have let your kind allowance, Papa, lay in my aunt's hands till this hat which I spoke for was brought home.

"As I am (as we say) a daughter of liberty, I chuse to wear as much of our own manufactory as pocible. But my aunt says I have wrote this account very badly. I will go on to save my money for a chip & a lining &c."

It was obvious that Nanny's aunt was also disturbed by the political cross-currents of the time. She certainly could not have approved of the daughter of a King's officer writing to him as "a daughter of liberty." But that part of their dilemma was settled a few months later. June 7, 1772, to the vast delight of Nanny, her family returned to Boston from Nova Scotia. Somehow, her father had brought about his severance from the Royal Army, and the family was going to live at the Winslow farm nearby in Marshfield.

Nanny did not pay particular attention to her diary

once her people were home. A lot of her entries were pretty short. She wrote on August 18:

"Many avocations have prevented me keeping my journal so exactly as heretofore, by which means a pleasant visit to the peacock. . . ."

Then, August 27:

"Yesterday I heard an account of a cat of 17 years old, that has just recovered of the meazels. This same cat is said had the small pox 8 years ago!"

She did not appear too much shaken by this piece of information, because she wrote calmly enough on a later date in the month:

"Very busy all day. Went into the common in the afternoon to see training. It was very prettyly perform'd."

Nanny was just about to close up the diary. Her entries in it had been infrequent for the last months, almost a year. But they were much happier in tone than in the past. She wrote on May 31, 1773:

"Monday last I was at the factory to see a piece of cloth cousin Sally spun for a summer coat for unkle. After viewing the work we recollected the room we sat down in was Libberty Assembly Hall, otherwise called factory hall, so Miss Gridley & I did ourselves the Honour of dancing a minuet in it."

The two young misses in their long dresses, frilly

pantalettes and neat black patent leather slippers must have made quite a sight as they danced across the wide floor of the hall without music. Nanny Winslow's health must have been better this year, too, and she was very pleased that the family was ready to leave Boston for the farm at Marshfield.

She finished with the diary on the same day, May 31, in a second entry:

"Dear Mamma, what name has Mr. Brent given his son? something like Nehemiah, or Jehoshaphat, I suppose. It must be an odd name. (our head indeed, Mamma.) Aunt says she hopes it a'nt Baal Gad, & she also says that I am a little simpleton for making my note within the brackets above, because when I omit to it, Mamma will think I have the help of somebody else's head, but, N. B. for herself, she utterly disclames either her head or hand concern'd in this curious journal, except where the writing makes it manifest. So much for this matter."

Nanny Winslow went to the big, white clapboard house at Marshfield with her family in the early summer of 1773, and she never left it. She adored the place, and passed many peaceful, pleasant hours there. A bit of sewing in her hands, or a book, she sat in the shade of one of the huge maple trees on the lawn and

looked out over the fields that stretched in the summer heat haze to the Marshfield River.

Oxen lowed and grunted as they hauled in the massive hay wains towards the barns. The sharp cries of the ox-herds, "Gee, thar! Haw, you, haw!" awoke the barn swallows. They flew twittering across the lawn, then settled down again in the shadows under the eaves. Along the river bank, boys who fished for carp and bullheads shouted to each other in triumph as a fish was pulled ashore, and the sounds came to Nanny oddly flattened through the haze. Bees droned around her, and a family cat, too lazy to chase birds, lay in sleep at her feet. Maybe Nanny drowsed where she sat, but it was more probable that she rested wide-awake, and wondered about her family's future.

A number of their Marshfield neighbors were moving out, going to Canada, to Nova Scotia, or back to England. The question was asked more and more, who was Tory, and who was for the Liberty Boys? Her father could not help but recall his years of service to the King, and it was no secret in Marshfield about what he would do if war really came. Without a doubt, he would rejoin the Royal forces, fight to keep the colonies loyal to the Crown.

The family stayed at Marshfield that winter, and in December there was the Boston Tea Party, and war became inevitable. Nanny's father finally left, his Tory feelings too strong to be taken by the people who opposed him. He went to England, and then to Quebec, resumed his duties as Commissary General in the Royal Army.

Nanny and her mother stayed on with a couple of servants in the big house. This was the place that Daniel Webster was to own later and to love so much. Still, for Nanny Winslow during the long, dark and fierce winters, it must have seemed like a prison. Her little brother, John Henry, had died, and her own health was steadily worse. She kept close to her room for weeks at a time while her fits of coughing increased, tore at her frail body.

Her mother reluctantly brought her word of Lexington, and of the other battles in the war. They must have often prayed together, and sung hymns, for letters from Nanny's father were rare. He was separated from his family for five years, and Nanny and her mother were very much alone.

Nanny was dying of tuberculosis, and there was nothing to be done for her. Each winter battered away more of her strength. It was so cold once that Mrs. Winslow wrote in her journal, "My bazon of water froze on the hearth with as good a fire as we could make in the chimney."

Mother and daughter remained together most of Nanny's waking hours. It must have been that her mother sang, and not always the stern Puritan hymns. There was one beautiful lullaby that came from Nanny's childhood:

"Sweet was the song the Virgin sung,
"When she to Bethlehem was come,
"And was delivered of her Son,
"That blessed Jesus hath to name,
"Lullaby, sweet Babe quoth she,
"My son and eke a Savior borne,
"Who hath vouchsafed from on high,
"To visit us that were forlorne,
    "Lulla, Lulla,

"Lullaby, sweet Babe sang she,
"And sweetly rockt him, rockt him, rockt him,
"And sweetly rockt him on her knee."

Anna Green Winslow died in the fall of 1779 at
Marshfield. There is no town or church record to mark
her death, or a headstone to mark where she was
buried. These were war years, and Marshfield was
an unhappy place. It was very probable, though, that
at the end she was ready to welcome death, and not
suffer another winter and further agony.

Her family remembered her a long time, and her
friends, and anybody who ever had the chance to read
her diary. She seemed to dance on and on in that
minuet without music in "Libberty Assembly Hall." A
small smile was at the corners of her mouth, and her
feet kept perfect rhythm.

GARDINER'S ISLAND, at the end of Long Island Sound off the coast of Connecticut, has a peculiar place in American history. There is no other island property like it which has been owned so long, and continuously, by one family. It is held at present by the direct descendants of Lion Gardiner, the man who established his title with a Montauk tribal sachem, Lord Stirling, and King Charles.

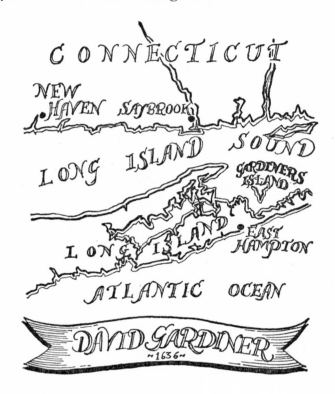

Chapter 3

BELOVED ISLAND

David Gardiner was less than two years old, yet he
sensed the danger. His family and the garrison of the
fort were under sharp attack. Big, red-headed Lion
Gardiner, his father, had been wounded in the fighting outside. He could just barely drag himself back
over the drawbridge, send it high on its chains before
the Pequot braves followed him.

Now David's mother began to pull the arrow shaft
from the wound. David wanted to cry as he watched
his father shudder with pain. But crying was only for
small babies, and he was past that. He kept very still
before he wandered off through the bluish gray powder smoke in the great main hall.

His mother was too busy to notice that he was gone
from her side. She had her husband to tend, and the
soldiers to supply with fresh powder horns and bags of
shot. The action would be decided in the next few
minutes.

The log-walled fort reverberated to the thump of the heavy muskets and the blows of the Pequots as they tried to ram a log through the single, very stout door. David Gardiner must have been almost numb with fright as he poked across the floor among the smoke eddies. But he stopped behind one of his father's soldiers, curiosity greater than fear.

The man stood at a loop-hole firing his bulky matchlock. David peered around him and looked up and saw at astonishing close range the face of a Pequot warrior.

The warrior held a fire brand. He was about to thrust it in through the long, narrow loop-hole. His crimson-striped face, shiny with bear fat, was drawn tight as he gave a warwhoop. Then, though, the whoop became a gargled, thick cry, and the face disintegrated, disappeared from before the loop-hole. The soldier had fired the matchlock, and David Gardiner had seen his first man killed.

The fight at Saybrook Fort was February 22, 1638. It was the beginning of the merciless Pequot war. David, who had been born in the fort in April, 1636, was to witness many scenes of sudden, violent combat before he was in his teens and able to handle a musket.

The February day of the attack when his father was wounded stayed in David's mind. His father would

not let him forget it, nor his mother. It should be, they both said, a most valuable lesson to him. David could only agree.

He had deep love for his parents, and enormous respect for his father. Lion Gardiner, a professional soldier since he had left England in his early youth, had served as a master sergeant of engineers in Sir Edward Vere's company in the Lowland wars. Then he had been hired by the wealthy backers of the Connecticut colony to come here in 1635 and build and command this fort.

It was on a small hill that rose from a neck of land where the broad, lovely Connecticut River flowed out into Long Island Sound. The Indians had a name for the place, Pashbehauks. But the English called it Saybrook after two of the noblemen who were shareholders in the company that backed the colony. The fort was built of square-hewn timber, with a moat and a palisade. Salt marshes and sandy beaches were all around it, and just beyond them groves of fine trees.

David Gardiner spent his first few years within the

palisade. His mother would not let him go any further until she was fully certain that he was to be trusted. Indians fired at any time upon the people from the fort. Warriors waited motionless for hours in the forest and then let go arrow after arrow. They shot men who mowed the marsh hay, or worked in the corn patches. They took cows as targets, and the soldiers' dogs, anything that moved and belonged to the hated white enemy.

David knew that the river was full of fish, and clams, and oysters, and mussels and crabs and eels. He saw soldiers from the garrison when they were off duty go down and catch them. And other men, who were more skillful and daring, went into the forest to hunt and came back with deer and partridge and rabbit. They shot geese and duck over the marshes, and swore that the local Pequots were really friendly, meant no harm.

But Lion Gardiner did not accept that statement. He trained David to watch the forest constantly for signs of Indians. Then, in August, 1638, when David's sister Mary was born, he was put a great deal on his own. His mother was simply too occupied with the new baby and all of her other duties and chores.

David scrabbled around during the sunny summer months, dug for worms inside the palisade, inspected beetles and flies and garter snakes, adopted lizards and a turtle. Still, he remembered what his father had told him. He climbed up every hour or so onto the footwalk along the palisade wall. He crouched behind a firing slit, and gazed at the forest, marking how a blue jay jabbered happily, squirrels chased after pine cones, and a fish hawk floated slow and silent across the currents of air above the river.

If there were Indians near in the forest, David told himself, the blue jay would stop jabbering. The squirrels, too, would be still. The hawk might keep on, high up there, but it was as fierce as the Pequots, and as unfriendly. David must have felt pretty content with himself after he had spent time on lookout like that. He probably went in the fort and begged a cooky from his mother, took a quick peek at his sister, and admired her, even though she was a girl.

David was charged with the care of Mary just as soon as their mother was sure that he could take responsibility. Her cradle was carried out from the fort while David played at his games beside the palisade. He kept the flies from her, saw that she did not get too much sun, and told her she should be ashamed of herself when she cried. But then, about a year after Mary was born, the family left the fort.

Lion Gardiner was through with being a mercenary

soldier, and under orders to other men. His contract with the Connecticut Company was finished. One of the proprietors of the company, a wealthy aristocrat named George Fenwick, had come to Saybrook Fort with his wife, two aunts and a number of servants. Gardiner wanted no part of such life.

He took his wife and David and Mary and put them aboard a boat with their belongings. Then he started off on a life wholly his own. He had secured the rights both from the agent for Lord Stirling, the English proprietor, and from the local Indian sachem to a fine, heavily wooded island only a few miles away across Long Island Sound from Saybrook. But the island would be his, his alone, and he and his family would live there in complete independence.

David was greatly thrilled as he heard his father describe it. Someday, if he lived long enough and became really smart, he would take his father's place and come to own the island in his turn. There was in between, he realized, a tremendous amount of work to be done. The island had never been lived on before by white people.

David went at the work happily, almost with outright joy. He and the entire family were at once immensely attracted to the island. Lion Gardiner called it Isle of Wight, after the famous island off the English coast. It was less than ten miles in length, but with many coves and salt and fresh water ponds, and a magnificent spread of forest across a great part. The nearest land was about twelve miles away, at a place the Indians called Acabonack. When the wind blew hard, or the dreaded banks of fog closed in, the Gardiner family were stuck on their island, completely isolated from the rest of the world.

But the family had made friends with the local Indians, the tribe that named themselves Manhansets and had once lived here, now occupied Shelter Island, off a few miles to the south. Lion Gardiner had also made a life-long friend of the most important sachem in all of the Long Island Sound region. He was Wyandanch, chieftain of the powerful Montauk tribe that lived in stout-walled log and bark wigwams on nearby Montauk Point and received tribute from the ten other tribes in the region. Wyandanch and his very intelligent squaw, Aswaw, were often on the Gardiner's island and stayed for long visits, and it was with Wyandanch that Lion Gardiner had found this place, decided to live here.

David came to know the tall, powerfully built and handsome sachem very well. Wyandanch taught him how to use an Indian bow, fire an arrow and correct the range for windage. His sister Mary, out of the baby stage and getting to be long-legged, watched for a while in awe and then went off to be instructed by Aswaw. The chieftain's wife showed Mary Gardiner how flax could be plucked from the plants in the fields, and a very, very small crab flipped from a salt water pool at low tide, held in the hand until he tickled too much.

The children lost a large share of their fear of Indians. They were taken by their parents to visit Wyandanch's principal village on the highlands of Montauk Point where, just beyond, the great Atlantic rollers slammed and boomed. They watched the sure-handed old braves make wampum from the famous dark purple quahaug clam shells, and the arrow-makers at work, slowly, deftly chipping flint, and the squaws who cut buckskin garments, stitched together marvellous feather head-dresses that the warriors wore at powwows, and the young girls who faithfully pounded kernels of corn into what the Indians called samp, a coarse kind of flour.

More than anything else, though, David and Mary were thrilled by the canoe passage from their island to Montauk, and back again. The canoes were big, made of fire-hollowed logs, and paddled by as many as eighteen warriors. Wyandanch sat aft, at the steering position, Lion Gardiner beside him. The warriors

chanted as they maintained stroke. Their reddish-brown skins gleamed under the high summer sun, and the eagle feathers in their brow circlets bobbed to the motion, and drops fell in quick little spurts of jewel colors from the blade tips. The passage never seemed long in Wyandanch's canoe; he used picked warriors as crew.

David and Mary, eager to leave their island for a visit, were always extremely happy to get home. Now, in September of 1641, they had a sister, Elizabeth, born here. She took their interest, and yet there was so much to be done, to be seen, that often from early breakfast until after supper at candle lighting time at dusk they were outside, held by various tasks, and, quite frequently, games they had invented for themselves. They knew the island thoroughly, from one end to the other. But it seemed that each day they must explore again some part of it.

Sweet water ponds and lakes were scattered along

the length. Then there were the great, fine stands of timber, and the meadows where Lion Gardiner had put his flocks of sheep, his herd of cows and his several horses to graze. Tall deer with wide racks and bright white scuts were in the oak forest in the western part, went delicately leaping away when David clapped his hands or Mary went, "Beep, beep!"

The corn land was to the south, and there, David knew, his father would in time build a windmill. Pumpkins lay plump yellow next to the tasseled corn in the early fall, and beside what Lion Gardiner called Tobacco Lot Pond the Indians grew the stuff they smoked in their stone-bowled pipes. The Indians also burned off the marsh grass and weeds to rid the island of the ticks that could cause so much trouble to the domestic animals. When the moon was on the wane, it meant that the tide was high, and so they swept the marshes with wooden rakes, took quantities of salt into their birchbark buckets.

Mary plucked flax for David in the way Aswaw, the wife of Wyandanch, had shown her. She promised to make him a shirt of it, and he said, all right, he knew where the clay pits were. He would make her a doll of clay, and give it a horsehair wig. She would have to make the dress, though, and find the name. That was girl stuff.

The Gardiner children lived a busy but a quite idyllic life during the months when they were not kept inside by the weather. Then they were no longer carefree, and could not wander most anywhere they wished. The feeling that they were at least part Indian was gone, and the terrible fear of attack had returned.

The big, strong, two-story house that Lion Gardiner had built and surrounded by a stockade was reasonably safe. The Pequot War was over, the Pequots almost exterminated as a tribe. But there were bands of tough Narragansett braves who came from Block Island across the winter sea at night under cover of the fog or snow. The passage was only about fifteen miles for them, and Gardiner's Island made an attractive target. It offered them many kinds of loot, and the chance at vengeance and scalps. White men, soldiers of the Massachusetts Bay Colony, had landed on Block Island and burned the Indian villages there, looted, slaughtered, and the Narragansett braves were very eager to pay back the score.

Lion Gardiner and his men servants slept little during the winter nights of fog or snow. They patrolled the house and the stockade, muskets at the ready. David was not supposed to stay up with them, but he often did, sat nodding by the huge chimney-place, one eye propped open to watch the powder horns and shot bags, ready to leap up and help the men save his home and his beloved island.

The winter months, especially for the children, seemed to go on forever. Gales beat at the house. Trees creaked in torment in the forest, and moaned; limbs broke from them with the force of the frost, the weight of the snow. It was a severe chore to get to the stock in the outbuildings, supply the beasts with fodder and water.

The family lived around the main chimney-place most of the wintertime. When supper was finished, and after candle lighting, the servants joined them there, all except the men whom Lion Gardiner stationed on guard. The settles and chairs and stools were pulled close to the hearth, and quite inevitably, as the wind sprang roaring in the chimney and the fire leaped and formed weird successions of shadows, the talk came around to death and other grim topics.

But, David noticed, his father would not allow much discussion of what was too serious. Life was hard enough for all of them in this isolated, lonely place, and nearly every winter somebody among the small company of people here died from one cause or another. Still, talk of ghosts and elves and hobgoblins and werewolves was not forbidden. Such things, Lion Gardiner admitted, might well exist, and his sturdy

Dutch wife and the rest of the grown people present nodded their heads in agreement, and David and Mary sat rapt, lost in wonder, and scared, and yet not wishing that they were as small as Elizabeth and could sleep through these hours.

The voices of the wind and the water were discussed, and the signs of the sun and moon, stars and clouds, and the meanings behind the movements of birds, the baying of dogs. Goblins were described, and then fairies, and Mary leaned forward tensely, her eyes ashine as she listened. Robin Goodfellow, she learned, was also called Puck, and his cream bowl must always be set brimming full for him.

There were more, many of them. Pigwiggin gave

cramps to folks who were lazy, and to little girls who
forgot to make their beds or pick up their toys. Billy-
blind was from the North Country in England, and
he chuckled on the hearthstones of the cottages nearly
every night. "Here, too?" Mary Gardiner wanted to
ask, but caught her mother's glance, and understood
that a lot of what was being said would not be talked
about in broad daylight.

The wind swept on outside, snatching at the eaves,
sending the sparks of the fire in a new, wild dance.
It brought more description of the "little folk." Water
nixies gripped the ankles of the travellers who around
dusk tried to cross a stream at flood. Strange, small,
wizened people, with faces like walnuts, peered at
the hunters who dared to cross the moors alone at
dusk. Fairies, and elves, and sprites danced around
pools and below waterfalls.

Mary smiled as she heard that, and looked at David.
But he was listening wide-eyed to the story of the
"green man" who was found in Lochaber in Scotland.
This "green man" was seen only between daylight and
starlight, when in all truth a man of the region had
been killed. His green-colored counterpart did not belong to either heaven or earth. And again in Scotland,
women had actually seen the devil. He was dressed in
brown clothes; he wore a little black hat.

Mary could not listen to any more. She stumbled from her stool into her mother's arms, curled up in the familiar lap, and was asleep. But David still sat and listened. He was waiting for the Narragansetts. Already, in his head, he considered himself a man.

Spring began to make promises to the children along in late March and early April. The wind hauled around from the northeast to the south, to southwest. Rain gnawed at the snow banks piled against the stockade. Snow slid thudding from the roof, and the eaves let go their icicles. Each day, the sun was a bit higher through the small windows, and the house was warmer.

David was sent outside to work in knee-length cowhide boots, and Mary was jealous. She had to stay in and tend to Elizabeth, and David came back to tell her of the first flights of ducks over the ponds, and the majestic sweep of geese, far, far up, on their way to Canada. Robins perched on the stockade, even sidled over to take bread crumbs from Mary when she tempted them to the front door sill. Then the last of the snow was gone, and although the dooryard was still muddy, her mother let Mary play there and take Elizabeth out in her crib.

All of the men were busy with plowing and planting, with repairing roads and fences, and turning the flocks into the fields. Then they started up the wind-

mill that Lion Gardiner had built to grind his corn and
wheat, and they scraped, caulked and painted the
boats, put them in the water for the first trip of the
season to what they called "the main," but was really
the village of East Hampton, on Long Island.

David delighted in helping with the work on the
boats. He had been taught how to splice and rig, and
repair blocks and deadeyes, sew patches on the coarse
hemp sails. He wanted to be out here on the water, he
told himself, when the seals arrived, and Wyandanch's
warriors paddled over in their hunt for whale. East
Hampton was a nice place; he liked to visit it and
poke around in the shops, buy toffee for Mary and
himself, a piece of lace for his mother, a real English doll for Elizabeth, and meet people whom he did
not see every day. Still, along towards the end of
April, where he belonged was off Bostwick Bay, on
the westerly side of his father's island.

That was the most likely spot for the right whales
to show themselves as they cruised north from the
tropics. And the seals were sure to come ashore on the
rocks further in, clambering up with a waggle and plop
of their flippers, brown-spotted and funny-looking,
with faces oddly like dogs. The Montauks and the
Manhansets and the rest of the local tribes killed the
seals without mercy. They went onto the rocks after

them and crushed in the beasts' thin skulls with clubs.

David had no great liking for the kill. The pleasure for him was when the seals came by the hundreds past the boat in which he sat, bumping it with their snub noses, gazing at him from wide, unwinking brown eyes. He wanted some day to catch a pup, a baby seal about two or three weeks old. He would keep it back in Tobacco Lot Pond, and feed it with fish he caught himself, only let Mary play with it at certain times, and Elizabeth once a day.

But a pup was hard to catch, and as yet he had been unlucky. He did much better at whaling, and Wyandanch welcomed him in his canoe, and Lion Gardiner gave permission for David to join the hunt. The right whales did not seem to have any knowledge of danger as they swam slowly from seaward into Long Island Sound. The twin columns of spray they thrust into a glistening shower about fifteen feet above their blow-holes marked them for the hunters. Wyandanch gave a signal with his raised arm.

The big dugout canoes closed from each side. The harpooners stood spraddle-legged in the bow. They carried weapons tipped with bone and attached to line made from hemp. Floats fashioned from wood were secured to the lines. David Gardiner helped handle them, and clearly understood their purpose. When a harpoon had been driven into the whale and the whale dived, the floats would drag after him, keep him near the surface.

The Indian harpooners struck again and again, sending the hardwood harpoons into rough black hide, and through, into tender muscles and veins. Bellowing, rearing half out of the water in agony, the sixty foot whale tried to get away from pursuit. But he could not; he now lacked the strength. His blood stained the sea. The many dives and the repeated harpoon strokes had finished him.

Wyandanch gave another signal. The canoe crews grasped the lines that led from the harpoons. They hauled the whale into the shallows off Gardiner's Island. Then some of them went over the side, maneuvered the carcass up onto the beach.

It was about there that David lost his enthusiasm for whale hunting. The rest of the operation, as the carcass was cut and stripped and the braves swallowed great globs of raw blubber, made him slightly sick. He was content to go and find his sisters, hunt for wood pinks and violets, watch the ospreys rebuild their nests in the same dead trees they used each year.

Lion Gardiner and his wife and family had entered upon a very happy period in their lives. The island was flourishing. Wool from the flocks of sheep, flour turned out by the mill, cheeses from the island herd and clay taken out of the pits for pottery were all bartered, across the Sound in Saybrook or New London. The only articles the island people needed were sugar, tea and iron, and those Gardiner got in barter, as well as cash for some of what he produced.

He had become a quite well-to-do man. He added to his house from the splendid stands of white oak in Bostwick Wood, at the west end of the island. Each trip he made across the Sound, he brought back expensive gifts for his family. Elizabeth was his favorite when she reached the talk-and-walk age, and for her he got a saddle and bridle made in England, put them on a gentle, stubby pony raised on the island.

Elizabeth learned to ride well after just a few falls. She lent the pony often to Mary and to David, but it was her personal pleasure to ride the length of the island. She trotted him over the beach sand at low tide, and through the field lanes, and into the woods where chipmunks and squirrels skittered, and foxes slid away into the underbrush in a red-brown flash of motion. Then she would dismount and gather black walnuts, and acorns and chestnuts, tie them up in a corner of her skirt before she rode off home.

But she had to rub down and stable and water and feed the pony herself, and take care of the bridle and saddle. Her mother had chores waiting: wool to be carded, flax to be picked, and all sorts of sewing and mending. There was always, Elizabeth told herself, something to be done all the time on Gardiner's Island.

The strain of the winter months, though, had begun to tell on Lion Gardiner. He had been in possession of the island for fourteen years now, and while it had made him prosperous, he had come to accept his wife's belief that they should move the family to "the main." From time to time, when he had traded there, he had picked up pieces of land in East Hampton township. He liked the site of the village. The sandy soil gave good crops, and all around the village were the rich crops to be harvested from the sea. He could still hold onto his island, and David, if the lad wished, could live here later, have it as his own.

Still, Lion Gardiner waited, not fully convinced that he was right. His wife, quiet and gentle, and also strong-willed, finally got him to accept the idea in full. She told him in the privacy of their bedroom that his great favorite, Elizabeth, was in love, wanted to be married, and very soon. Lion Gardiner grunted, and smiled, and said, yes.

The Gardiners moved to East Hampton and built a tall white clapboard house. Elizabeth was fifteen, a good age to be married according to the standards of the time. Her husband was a young, husky Englishman named Arthur Howell who came from nearby Southampton. Rough old Lion Gardiner, a lot of gray in the red beard and hair, was pleased by his new son-in-law.

He gave the couple as a wedding gift a farm on his East Hampton property, and ten head of cattle. It was a magnificent gesture. David and Mary, who were to find mates soon themselves and marry, stood a bit awed when they heard of it. But David was thinking of the island out in the gleaming, wind-capped bay. His home was there, he knew, and he was about ready to go back.

David returned and took his family and servants. He became on Gardiner's Island just as much his own master as any manor lord in England. He left behind him all of the vexations and involved, prolonged disputes that seemed to be a permanent part of village life. He avoided the bitter talk about who owned what woods lot or field, and who had the right to graze cattle upon certain sections of the Common. The tithing man was left behind, too, and the snoops, the gossips, the noisy neighbors, the over-officious minor officials, and the minister with his long, difficult sermons.

More than anything else, though, David was the absolute and unquestioned master of the island. This was during a period when in England only a small part of the land was available for tillage, and it was being reduced because of the enclosure of the open fields and commons, the conversion of farms for the breeding of sheep. David, the son of a man of peasant birth, considered himself extremely fortunate.

There was certain, almost constant danger to be met on the island. He and his wife, his children and their descendants accepted it. They believed that it was worthwhile in exchange for their life of freedom.

Gardiners persisted on the island. They prospered there, and against every sort of adversity. Winter storms, snow, ice and hostile Indians isolated them for months at a time. There was fire, disease, disaster. Pirates infested the area towards the end of the seventeenth century. Captain William Kidd came ashore with a load of Indian Ocean loot and told the present owner, John Gardiner, to bury it and forget about it until he returned, else he would take John's head. But Kidd never came back, was hanged instead at Execution Dock, and the King's men from Boston called for the loot.

John Lyon Gardiner had a more general problem in his turn. He was the seventh owner in direct descent and he wrote in his diary in May, 1797:

"Wrote Esq. Cooper, am told you have but just now laid the keel for my boat. I am extremely disappointed that she is not finished especially since I gave you the urgent reasons there were for having her some time ago. Wish to know whether you mean to build her and when. Have nothing but a skiff and a week ago a woman put to bed, and yesterday a fine active boy of six years old died in one of the families—had no boat for a doctor."

David Gardiner began around 1770 the construction of the famous manor house with its fine, broad portico and dormer windows, great trees on each side as shelter from the sea wind. Whaleboats were sent off regularly for the catch during the season, and bonfires burned on the headlands as beacons for the crews. The record tells of 316 cows and oxen on the island at the time. There were almost 3,000 sheep, which "pastured on the downs," and wild turkeys came to be fed with tame fowl. David Gardiner had a force of nearly a hundred servants, many of whom were Negro slaves. He regarded himself as a manor lord, and lived like one, and maintained several carriages on the island for himself and his family and friends.

Then, August 8, 1775, a British fleet of thirteen vessels anchored off the northeast side of the island. Colonel Abijah Willard sent 200 red-coated soldiers ashore from the frigate *Rose* to gather provisions. The Gardiner family was in East Hampton; only an overseer, a Negro slave and a Montauk squaw were on the island. The British took off a number of cattle without much trouble in long boats, although they were forced to use three halters apiece to haul them aboard ship and broke the necks of some.

The British left, and returned, and Admiral Marriot Arbuthnot sent men onto the island to establish a base. Officers occupied the manor house, and treated it well enough. But troops were quartered in one of the farmhouses that was used as both a barracks and a hospital, and they nearly wrecked it. Winter and close confinement brought epidemic. The dead were buried in shallow graves all over the island, at Cherry Harbor, Bostwick Woods, Study Hill and Plumb Point.

With the end of the war, the Gardiners were back,

repaired the damage, set up again a regular way of life. They have kept it ever since, and probably will hold onto the island for some time to come. It is a rich heritage.

JOHN SCOTT was born into the same sort of circumstance as Henry Spelman. Like Henry, his people enjoyed upper-class prestige and were well-to-do. But, unlike Henry, the Cavalier colonel's son had no desire whatsoever to come out to the New World.

He was sent as a prisoner, brutally and stupidly banished by judges who had a small sense of justice, no feelings of humanity, and hatred of anybody, even an eleven-year-old boy, who opposed their political ideas. Banished from England for life, John had always one great dream: to return and clear his name and his family's name.

First, though, in Salem and the Massachusetts Bay Colony, he was subjected to weird and tragically confused experiences which left a profound impression on his life. Cavalier and a Catholic, he had been banished by Oliver Cromwell's nose-pinching Puritan judges during a time when Puritans savagely fought Catholicism and the King. Young John was better treated by the Roundhead cavalry—called so because of their round steel helmets—than by supposedly educated and gentle folk.

Salem taught him nothing except further reasons for hatred. He was sold by a Puritan to a family soon to be persecuted for Quaker beliefs. It is no wonder that in his mature years, although he gained the rank of colonel in the Dutch Army, John Scott was never quite sure of what he should do next, nor the basic purpose of his life.

Chapter 4

CAVALIER SLAVE

There were twenty of them, some precociously tough, a few already vicious and evil, and of the lot only John Scott was gentleborn. But he was just as desperate as the other boys. He was tall for his age, too, and strong, and after the first night at sea the bully who called himself the leader of the London urchins let John be, reconsidered his future with a broken nose.

John Scott lay in the wet, stinking dark of the ship's main hold and tried to keep the hammock from swinging too far. If it lurched widely again, he thought, he would surely be seasick, and he had enough now, lice, dysentery and the knuckles he had skinned on the London bully's nose. John was eleven years old, and around him in the hold he heard unrestrained weeping. He almost wept, then checked the impulse, turned on his side and slept.

He awoke to a gray, still wet dawn, but the hatch overhead was open, he saw, and a sailor who stood

there shouted down that they could come on deck. John clambered out and stretched and yawned and felt his extreme hunger and with it a sense of great excitement. He was on his way to the New World in this year of 1643, he told himself, and had better make what he could of the fact. The Puritan court in London had banished him to New England for life.

John moved alongside the bulwark of the low midships deck. He stood tense, breathless as the clumsy little ship rolled. *Seabridge* nearly put her beam-ends into the tumbling sweep of slate-green waves, righted herself only at the last moment. Sprays rushed aboard and a slosh of solid water from the wave crests. John was soaked to the knees but he did not mind that; his boots had been stolen from him in prison. A young

Cavalier rascal had no need for hand-made boots, the turnkey told him, and should go barefoot.

John laughed suddenly, his face lifted to the sprays. He liked to stand here barefoot, his toes gripped hard upon the deck planks, his shirt billowed from his body by the wind, his hair flung back from his face and the early spring sun brass-yellow yet on the horizon. He was a Kentish squire's son, he recalled, a country lad. Still, he had come to love the sea, and before he was through he would be a sailor. He released his hands from the bulwark and balanced himself, knees very slightly bent, to the surge, the pitch and roll and return of the ship. He swung, and looked around at her.

She resembled a badly contrived box, with the fore and after castles built up high from the ends of it, the two stub masts and their clutter of heavy rope rigging close together upon the main deck. Her square-cut sails were made of baggy yellow hemp, strained now to the gale that blew off Land's End. Back there was England, and from the sun's direction the course was Southwest. He felt very pleased when he heard one of the officers on the poop call to the steersman, "Hold her sharp Sou'west. 'Tis no barrel ye have to handle, but a ship!"

John peered at the steersman and did not envy him. The steersman crouched in a sort of half deck below

the poop and fought a long and constantly cranky til-
ler. His face was slick with sweat, and veins showed
blue, distended in his arms. Ten weeks to Salem, the
crew had said last night at Gravesend. Ten long weeks.
But on this April morning, unless he acted smart, he
would miss his breakfast.

The rest of the deported boys had lined up beside
the brick fireplace abaft the foremast. They carried
wooden bowls and they held them out to the cook for
their rations of pease porridge. John remembered his
own bowl, and scampered down the hatch after it. The
cook was still ladling porridge when he returned, and
just as he took his ration he saw Emmanuel Downing.

Downing was a wealthy Londoner, a lawyer and
former Attorney in the Court of Wards. He was greatly
interested in the Salem colony and at present made
his home there, and because of his work in the Court
of Wards had been put in charge of the group of deported boys. Downing, neatly dressed in somber
Puritan clothing, made an impressive figure as he
climbed the ladder from his private cabin to the quarter deck. John Scott was a gentleman's son, and grateful for the porridge. He bowed to Downing, and said,
"Good morning, sir."

One of the bigger Lambeth urchins sneered crooked-
mouth at John Scott. "Snatch a bit o' favor, hey? Fer-

get yer a Cavalier sod and tickle a Puritan genneman's back. Proper smart, orl right."

John Scott ate his porridge in silence; he was very hungry. Then he approached the Lambeth urchin and started to deal him a blow with the side of the bowl.

" 'Ere, now!" the cook yelled. " 'Ere, now! Wot's up?"

Emmanuel Downing had heard that up on the quarter deck. He talked shortly with the senior watch officer and indicated the group. The officer told them rough-voiced that they would be equipped by the bosun with brooms, shovels and buckets. They could spend their energy mucking out the cattle stalls in the lower hold.

John Scott reflected bitterly about his past as he pushed a twig broom between the lowing, moaning, glaze-eyed animals. Life had changed enormously for him, he realized, and for the worst. Nor would it be better for a long while.

The trouble had begun last year when his father, Colonel John Scott, had sold the family estate in Kent and put the sum of 14,300 pounds at the disposal of King Charles. The colonel was a devoted Royalist, a Cavalier willing to make any sacrifice to keep Charles on the throne. A few months later, leading a Cavalier squadron of cavalry on a routine patrol at Alford in

Hampshire, Colonel Scott was killed by a Roundhead trooper.

John Scott and his mother were left without a home and with very little to support them. His mother was deeply worried. The King's army was about to swing across the Thames River into Kent, and already men from Cromwell's force of Roundhead soldiers had begun to loot in the neighborhood. John and his mother went to London and took quarters there and Mrs. Scott believed that they would be safe.

But John spent a lot of his time in the streets. London fascinated him after the quiet of Kent, and London in wartime was a challenge. It was common talk that the King was ready to bring the royal army in to attack the city. Prince Rupprecht, the King's nephew, was in command of the Cavalier cavalry and was greatly feared. Cannon were being put in place at Temple Bar and on Tower Hill. Women and children were at work on fortifications at Piccadilly and Lambeth, and around Constitution Hill. The government needed 4,000 horses to meet the Cavalier threat.

John listened, and watched, and remembered how his father had died. His father had been a cavalryman, a very fine one. Now almost every private coach in London was being stopped, the horses taken from the traces by Roundhead troopers. Farm teams were requisitioned in the markets, and wagoners and carterers stood white-faced with fury as their animals were led off to be saddled and bridled as cavalry mounts.

Then on the night of November 12, the largest army ever assembled in England, Cromwell's Trained Bands of 24,000 men, started out of the city to intercept the royal army, attack and if possible destroy it. The men marched in a dense and acrid fog, westward, over the Old Bath Road. They were armed with pikes and halberds and matchlocks; the cavalry in their knee-high boots loomed huge, beads of moisture on their saber scabbards and casques and corselets. The horses moved at a slow trot, or a walk. It was not difficult for John Scott to keep up with them. His only weapon was a small pocket knife, but he had decided exactly the way he would use it. He was a Royalist, too, he told himself, just as much as Colonel John Scott had been.

The army marched through the night, the flaring torches dim in the fog, but bright upon the horses' eyeballs. Before dawn, and from the west, there was a sound that made the troopers sit up in the saddle. That was not thunder, John Scott knew; that was cannon fire. King Charles was close with the royal army. Some of the Cavalier light artillery was engaged with the Roundheads.

The tall, pale boy took the knife from his pocket. He opened it, and tried the blade. Soon, he promised himself, he would pay back the Roundheads a great deal.

The Trained Bands in column of route march came out onto Turnham Green just as the fog began to lift before noon. The cottages of the little village were to the rear of the force as it spread out over the common and unit commanders bawled orders. John Scott kept with the cavalry. He waited for the squadrons to deploy. There was no fighting yet, no attack, although across the common were the royal standard and the battle flags of the King's men.

A Roundhead colonel came at the canter past John Scott and shouted that the troopers were to dismount and picket their animals. The beasts should be kept fresh for combat, whenever that arrived. Picket ropes were stretched, and stakes pounded into the ground. John stood just a bit aside and watched, then, very slowly, moved in upon the picket line.

He murmured comfortingly to the horses as he slid among them, lifted a saddle so he could cut the girth, then slit the bridle. He had been raised with horses; his father had taught him how to keep them quiet. It was a pity that Colonel Scott could not see his son now; sixteen, seventeen, eighteen girths and bridles.

That meant eighteen Roundhead troopers would have to fight as infantry, and they would not do too well in those huge boots.

A huge boot suddenly caught John Scott from behind. He was knocked headlong, and kicked again, and picked up and beaten after the knife was taken out of his hand. A sergeant led him to a captain, then a major and a colonel. He was not beaten any more. The Puritan officers, stern-faced and quiet men, asked him questions in low voices. They did not seem surprised at what he had done. But the court in London where he was tried months later *banished him for life from England.*

His family had raised five hundred pounds for his defense. His mother had used all of the influence still within her power as the widow of a Cavalier colonel. Nothing changed the decision of the court, not even the fact that there had been no battle fought at Turnham Green, and the King's forces had withdrawn from the field. So eleven-year-old John was sent on his way to *Seabridge* and Salem, and he knew that never again would he see his mother after that last day of his trial.

Seabridge kept on her wallowing way across the Atlantic, and little by little John Scott's sense of desolation and loss disappeared. He had become accustomed to the ship, the sea, the urchins. This was part of his new life, and to look back did no good. He made friends with several of the Lambeth boys, and when the captain of *Seabridge* put the ship in at La Horta in the Azores for fresh stores and water, they went ashore together.

None of them had ever before seen a palm tree, or such high, verdant mountains. The pastel-colored town and the Portuguese men in their tight corduroy pants, knitted stockings and tasseled caps resembled gypsies at home and made the boys laugh until Mr. Downing curtly told them to be quiet.

They slipped away from Downing for more than an hour, though, and went baretail swimming off a black volcanic sand beach. There were ducking matches, and wrestling and foot racing on the beach before Downing caught up to them. Then they were assembled and marched to the boat that took them back to the ship.

Seabridge had an easier time after the Azores were astern. The weather was better and the gales were gone. John Scott worked on deck along with the crew whenever the bosun gave him permission. He was serious about learning a sailor's trade, and had begun to hope that he might somehow stow away aboard the ship, escape going into servitude in America.

But, with the Massachusetts coast close, the boys were herded onto the main deck and told by Downing to form a single file. They were passed before a bar-

ber, who clipped their shaggy hair, and two unfortunate urchins who suffered from hookworm and lice, were completely shaven and issued wigs to wear. The boys stared at each other and knew what this meant. They were to be sold as slaves in Boston, and now they were being fixed up so that they would look well for the future bidders. John Scott spit over the side, his mouth bitter with the taste of hatred. He detested the idea of being any man's slave.

The Massachusetts coast, the vast bay and the wooded, rugged islands made small impression upon him. His mind was filled with the thought that he was about to lose the final fragments of his freedom. Colonel John Scott's son, one of the Kentish folk who had served English kings proudly for generations, defended their country along the white chalk cliffs and out at sea, past the famous Cinque Ports. Now . . . John Scott did not weep; he used instead a foul curse word learned from his Lambeth friends.

It was just as bad as he had imagined at the public auction in Boston where they were sold. Long-nosed, tight-faced Puritans came up to them and pinched their biceps and their calf muscles, peered down their their throats, examined their teeth, their feet. The boys were sold one by one, and Emmanuel Downing took the money, tucked it into a leather saddlebag he carried. John Scott rested rigid, his hands at his side, his eyes almost shut. Which one of these Puritans would pick him, he wondered, and lead him off like a cow from a county fair? But then Downing beckoned to him and said, "Step over yon, John Scott. You go with me to Salem, 'Tis not for you here."

John felt better then, and almost gay. Salem was a port town, he had heard, and all around it was the forest. If he could not get aboard a ship he'd slip off into the forest. By fall and cold weather, he would know his way around, and probably be living with a tribe of red Indians.

He told none of this to Downing or to Downing's servant when they left Boston the next morning. The servant had arrived from Salem with a pair of horses, and John rode pillion behind the man. Downing led the way on his mount, still very proper in his black broadcloth and narrow-brimmed Puritan hat, the money-bulged saddlebag at his knee. John had both contempt for Downing and a feeling of curiosity about the man. There were times when Downing acted almost human, seemed to forget the bleak tight prejudices of his religious beliefs; he smiled once in a while and hummed a tune, even if it was a hymn, and talked with the servant about the decoy ducks he had brought from England as an innovation.

John listened and stared at the rough trail and into the huge, gloomy and majestic forest. He had already begun to change his plans about living there. The man servant reported to Downing stories of wolves that had snatched a heifer right on Salem Common, and cougars and bears and panthers who raided the unwary in wintertime. There were many streams to be forded along the way, and John clung hard to the lanky servant's midriff, nearly slid from the horse's rump.

It took two days to reach Salem from Boston along the trail. John was reassured when he saw the compact little town on its rocky promontory that thrust forth into the reaches of Massachusetts Bay. He had just come to the firm conviction that he did not own any real pioneer spirit. Let the Indians keep the forest. He had seen, or he had imagined he had seen, enough wild animals during the trip to make him a townie. He would stay right in Salem, no matter what, until he could get aboard a ship. There were no black bears, no cougars or panthers at sea, and he'd trust to his luck with sharks.

Now he gave all his attention to the town. He felt almost as much dread as curiosity. Here was where he must work out his term of servitude, and he would be reminded often of his past. Salem resembled in many respects the seaports he had known at home in Kent.

The houses along twisting Essex Street were neatly whitewashed, gabled in the Tudor style, and with the second stories jutting out from the first. The town common was about half swamp, and the beaches littered with pebbles and great granite boulders. The cattle grazing on the common seemed in good shape, there were many "cent shops" in the lower front rooms of the Essex Street houses, and from the waterfront came the steady rap and tap of caulking hammers, the sounds of saws and planes and adzes. Salem was busy building vessels, and at the wharves were shallops and pinnaces, a few ketches, a bark and a lot of tippy-looking craft that John recognized as dugout canoes.

Fort Pickering, which John had heard Downing's servant describe as recently finished, lay at the end of a causeway on Winter Island. The walls, the corner guard-towers, the gate were all of logs, and he could see the soldiers at sentry-go along the footwalks, muskets at the ready. So the Indian troubles weren't over yet, John told himself, and there was another reason for him to stay away from the forest.

An Indian wearing a dirty buckskin breechclout, a droopy feather in his hair and the odor of rancid bear grease sidled past the horses in the street. The horses shivered a bit and stared nervously aside at the brave, and John wrinkled his nose. The brave smelled worse than the Lambeth urchins.

But the town took his attention again, and he felt no further curiosity about the Indian. The white and prim, square-built First Church was in front of them and John stared at it with a speculative glance. He had learned a bit about Puritan habits aboard *Seabridge,* and certainly he would spend most of each Sunday perched on a hard pew bench in the meeting-house. Next to the church, and put there deliberately by the General Court to stress the importance of good, clean religious thought were the whipping post, the bulky, heavy wooden stocks, and the pillory. The stocks were empty, and the blood on the whipping post was dark, stale. Three people, two men and a woman, stood in the pillory, though, and their tongues were jammed between the clefts in sticks.

"Them folk yon," Downing's servant said, "are declared liars. Court proved 'em such."

" 'Tis still a poor way," John Scott said, "to make people pay for a small sin."

The servant half-turned in the shallow saddle. He squinted at John. "Talk like that will put ye right beside them," he said. "And you shut up, instanter. I don't want no such talk roundabouts me."

John Scott had a lot he wanted to say in answer, but he sat silent. Downing had also swung to take a look at him, and in the street several men in severely plain Puritan clothing had halted. They nodded in recognition to Downing, and one said in a flat voice, "Who is the lad, pillion with Caleb?"

"A bound boy," Downing said. "He's to be sold here. He shall soon pick up our manners."

"You—" John Scott began, and stopped. He pretended a fit of coughing instead, and brought his heels so hard against the belly of the servant's horse that the beast broke into a lope along the street and left Downing and his Puritan friends behind.

Bound boy, John Scott said to himself. Bound boy, for sale. . . . They'd sell their own mothers, these folk, and they must have hearts of stone.

But Downing's servant had reined in the horse and dismounted. "Get ye down, too, bound boy," he told John Scott. "And watch out. 'Tis Governor Winthrop's sister our master is married to, and a strict one she is. You'll fetch up sure at the whippin' post, keep on as you are."

John Scott put his finger to the end of his nose in an indelicate gesture. He knew better than to make any other reply, though; Downing came along the street, and the front door of the big, pleasant house where they had halted was open. A woman in unmistakable Puritan dress stood in the doorway and gazed narrow-eyed at him. That must be Downing's wife, John Scott thought, and for a Puritan she looked quite pretty, and human.

John was well-treated that day and that night in the Downing's home. He shared the family supper, and after a long night of sleep was given a roast pigeon breakfast that exactly suited his fancy. A good part of his anxiety left him; he believed that somehow Downing had changed his mind, was not going to sell him. But then Downing nodded at him, and indicated that they should go together from the house.

John followed the man at the three pace distance he had discovered was correct for master and servant. He had the despairing hope that at the last moment he might shame Downing into keeping him. Downing had sons of his, John's age, whom he kept in England. John had found it out last night; the Downings did not want their boys in a place like Salem because here their education would suffer and they would become backward. Downing must know about him, have some amount of pity, compare John with his own sons and think a bit about his education which would suffer so much if he were to be sold as a slave.

Still, Downing went along Essex Street without even looking around at him. He stopped before a substantially built house where a large, thick-bodied man greeted him with the "thees" and "thous" of a Quaker. Then the Quaker studied John coldly and speculatively, and at last told Downing, "Taken. Give me the papers to sign."

"But you must teach the lad to read and write," Emmanuel Downing said. "And if you're to keep him 'til he's twenty-one, he shall be instructed also in the mastery of a trade. Agreed?"

"These things I agree to do," the Quaker said. He glanced again at John. "Tell me thy name, lad."

"John Scott," John said, his voice sharp-edged with rage. "What's yours?"

Both men scowled at him, and then the Quaker said, "Mine is Lawrence Southwick. But thou shall call me 'master,' and at once thine head shall be cropped, to teach thee humility and to show that thou are my servant."

"Yes, master," John said defiantly, and glared from him at Downing. "A fine pair of Christians, you two."

"The next thing for you, lad," Downing said in a

level voice, "is the whipping post. You must learn to hold your tongue in this place. Go now with your new master. Let us pray that he is patient with you, and Goodwife Southwick the same."

John was so furious, and so filled with shame that he was beyond speech. He entered flush-faced, stumbling into the house at Southwick's order and in the spacious, shadowy main room met the rest of the family. Mrs. Southwick appeared gentle and sweet-natured, and not at all the kind who would buy a boy like a market animal. There were five children, from John, the eldest, who was twenty-three, down to a little girl in a pinafore whose name was Provided. But Southwick did not waste any time on John Scott, or tell him more about the family. He ordered John to kneel and stay still, then clipped his hair almost to the scalp; this was the outward sign that John was an indentured servant, at the absolute bottom of the social scale in Salem and anywhere in the American colonies.

John locked his teeth and kept still when Emmanuel Downing returned with the indenture papers. There was nothing he could do, he knew. Not now, at least. He must wait, learn about the town, and much more about the sea. Then there would be a ship that would take him away from Salem forever.

He was greatly relieved when he found that

Lawrence Southwick held the quite important job of Town Cowkeep. That meant he would be on the common all day long, tending the people's stock. He would have a chance to wander away occasionally, and get down to the waterfront, make friends with sailors, some mate, and maybe the captain of a ship that ran to the Spanish Main. Once on the Main, he could take up with the buccaneers, make his fortune in one great, bold raid upon a Spanish ship or fortress town jammed with gold.

"Come along now, thee," Southwick said harshly to him. "Enough of day-dreaming. Thee shall lose the cattle to the Indians or the wolves, if not smart about the herding. Take yon goad. Use it freely. The cows must learn that thou are their master."

"Like you are mine," John Scott said, some of the rage still burning deep.

Southwick nodded and did not smile. "Aye," he said.

John Scott spent the next five years in servitude to the Southwick family. He came after a time to have a reluctant admiration for the couple, and quite an affection for the younger children. Southwick and his wife, Cassandra, kept the articles of the indenture agreement and taught John to read, write and cipher, and the younger children, in particular Daniel and little, cheery Provided treated him as a member of the family. He was given help with his cow-tending chores, and after supper with all of the other chores common in any colonial household.

Supper was served early, usually before candle light was needed in the great main room. It was almost invariably *samp,* Indian corn meal boiled and tasteless and thin. There might at rare intervals be *hotch-potch,* again an Indian word, for what meant stew, and perhaps twice or three times a year a little meat roasted on the fireplace spit. Then the wooden trenchers, the long-handled horn spoons and the cooking pot were put away, and the whole family began to work.

Hemp and wool were carded by Mrs. Southwick and her daughters, and made into articles of clothing. Lawrence Southwick fashioned out boots and shoes from cowhide, guided his sons and John Scott in the manufacture of chairs, tables, axe helves, flails, goads, all kinds of necesary equipment. The only break from this routine was the hours devoted each evening to Bible reading, and the lessons for the younger children and John.

John almost forgot the happiness, the gaiety of his early life in England. The country fairs back in Kent had been great occasions for dancing, singing, the playing of games. Here a boy, especially one under indenture, was forbidden to have anything to do with a girl. Christmas was not observed, and nearly all of the other holidays were ignored by the Puritans as being ungodly.

John came to look forward to the eight days of militia training each year when at least he could get away from dour, nasty-spirited Salem. The militia company camped out, and boys from the age of ten years up were trained in the use of bows, and matchlocks and half-pikes. They stood guard, and patrolled the camp, hauled wood for the fires. Still, the sergeant saw that they got a bit of free time to lope over to the Neck at Marblehead and go for a swim in the summer sea while the tide whooped in and splattered fifty-foot waves over the boulders.

John dreaded Sunday, not only because for hours on end he was forced to listen to two sermons. He realized as he grew older that the Southwick family had become more and more open in their denial of Puritanism and fervent in their Quaker beliefs. It would certainly bring tragedy for them, and for him also, in a lesser way, as their chattel.

Lawrence and Cassandra Southwick now refused to attend church, and that was a grave violation of the laws of the colony. They were repeatedly fined, and then whipped, and pilloried, and, after them, their children. But none of them would give up the "inward light" which was the central, guiding factor of the religion practiced by the members of the Society of Friends.

There was no such thing as religious freedom here, John Scott realized. He was tall and strong for his age, tanned by the outdoor life he led. The town people had long ago accepted him, admired his skill with cattle, looked upon him as the next Cowkeep since the Southwicks had entered into so much serious trouble. But John could remember his own past, and the irony it contained.

His father, a Catholic and a Cavalier, had been killed by Roundhead Protestants. So he, loyal to his father's memory and his father's king, had tried a wild trick to help the royalist cause, been caught and in a Protestant court been banished from his homeland for life. Protestant had sold him to Protestant in Salem, and now they fought among themselves, and he was the loser.

Lawrence Southwick could no longer keep him. The man had been fined so much that he was broke, and desperate. He petitioned the General Court in December, 1647 that John be allowed to be put on sale "as per covenant with Emmanuel Downing." The court, after deliberation, answered Southwick. It ordered him to "put forth said Scott for three years to any honest man."

John Scott did not need any more than that. He knew that Daniel and Provided Southwick, to show their sympathy with their parents' beliefs, had stayed away from church and been heavily fined. When the children said they had no money to meet the fines, the General Court ordered them sold as slaves to the West Indian plantations.

But there was no shipmaster in the port who would carry out the order. All of them refused to deport the children to work in the sugar cane fields where their life expectancy was less than a year. John Scott took hope from the fact. He slipped away from the bailiffs who kept a watch these days over the Southwick house. He got down to the town wharf and talked there with a captain whose ship was about to sail.

John Scott realized a great dream and went off to sea that night. He spent six months in the Caribbean, sailing among the mountainous, green-shouldered islands, learning a new vocabulary, and a whole new way of life. But the ship in which he served was owned in Salem. The captain warned him that he must return there. John only nodded. He had reckoned it; this dream was too fine to last.

The ship came into Salem in May, 1648. There were bailiffs on the dock, and they recognized John, hustled him ashore to the jail. He did not fight them, or protest, or argue. During the past few years, he had learned patience along with his reading, writing and ciphering.

He was sent to Boston by the town authorities, and tried before the General Court. One of the members of it was Emmanuel Downing, and he closely studied the powerfully built young lad in the wide-bottomed cotton trousers and sleeveless sailor's shirt. The decision of the court was that John be assigned back to Lawrence Southwick. His indenture was to be extended for the exact number of days he had been gone, and he must also pay his owner the sum of thirty-five shillings, the cost of the trial.

John stood straight to hear the sentence. Downing as he watched him must have reflected that his sons had received a much different education. But, along the way, John Scott had learned a great deal more. He would be free by law at twenty-one. Then he would go far beyond them, become a better man.

DURING THE more than one hundred years of French-Indian warfare along the northern colonial frontiers, the most terrible ordeal other than being burned at the stake was the captive march into Canada. Most of the women and children subjected to it failed to reach the French settlements. They died along the way, or were quickly murdered as their strength left them.

Still, dozens and sometimes scores survived each march, usually about 300 miles long and three to four weeks in duration. Most of the marchers were women and children; the men had been killed off back in the settlements, or escaped into the forest or a "stronghouse" where they had been able to defend themselves. The prisoners were sold in Canada, and then the majority of them disappeared forever.

Those who were bought from their owners and returned home were often more Indian in their habits than English. A number of them chose to stay in Canada; they liked the easy-going Indian life, pre-

ferred the gay and vivid French to the dour, repressed people at home.

Religious differences meant very little to young children, no matter what their upbringing. Eunice Williams cannot be severely blamed for her change in loyalties. It is not surprising that after what happened to her she was happy to marry a Caughnawaga brave. For the brave to take her name of Williams as a sign of honor is most unusual. And that she insisted he accompany her home to Deerfield with their children, not once but several times.

He must have been a courageous man. There were certainly people in Deerfield who had long memories. He risked the chance as a brave, a detested "Tawny," of being scalped, or shot out of old vengeance.

There is no other spectacle more appealing in colonial history than Eunice Williams, the grown woman, in a dress worn for the first time in years, on her way across Deerfield Common accompanied by her family and also her husband, to hear her father preach. Here mercy was not strained, and forgiveness was more than a word rattled forth from the pulpit. Eunice had come back to Deerfield and found peace.

Chapter 5

BLANKET SQUAW

It was so cold when Eunice went to bed that she jumped in with all her clothes on, and her mother had already allowed her to use the warming pan. She shucked off her clothes piece by piece under the blankets, pitched them out to the chair beside the bed. Her feet wrapped in the bottom folds of her flannel nightgown, she snuggled deep, pulled the pillow high and was at once asleep.

Eunice was seven years old, and one of the eight children of the Reverend John Williams and his wife. They lived in Deerfield, in the northwestern part of Massachusetts, and that village, in the winter of 1704, was the last, isolated outpost on the border. Beyond, to the North, was Indian country, occupied by various tribes who hated the English colonists, and were incited to great cruelty by their French allies, the masters of Canada.

Danger was constant for the settlers who lived

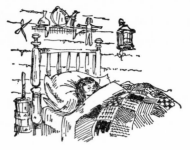

like the folks in Deerfield along the Connecticut River. There had been repeated raids in the past against Northampton, Hadley, Springfield and Deerfield itself. Back in 1675, when the congregation was about to go into the church on Sunday morning, Indians sprang out of the long grass of the Deerfield meadows. A man too slow to take protection inside the church was chased by the braves, caught in a swamp, scalped and killed, and another was wounded before he could get away. Soon afterward, ten people were killed in Northfield when trapped in an ambush.

So a company of eighty troops under Captain Lathrop was assigned as guard when on September 18, 1675 carts carrying corn and other supplies were sent from Deerfield to Hadley. The teams hauling the carts did not move fast. It was a magnificent early fall day with sunlight shimmering over the valley meadows, and the grapes ripe on the vines beside the road. Most of the men in the guard company were young, husky farmers called up for duty from Essex County. They liked the grapes, and stopped to gather handfuls of them where the road reached the ford at Bloody Brook.

The Indians fired the first volley while the militiamen had clusters of grapes in their hands and mouths. Then they closed in from the underbrush, and worked with the hatchet, the scalping knife. Bloody Brook, roiled with mud by the struggles of desperate and dying men, turned red. Only seven, at best eight of Captain Lathrop's company survived the ambush.

Reverend Williams knew the details of these raids when he brought his family to live at Deerfield and took over the pulpit for the 268 people in the village. He was a resolute and strong man, a Harvard graduate born at Roxbury who had preached the Protestant faith for nearly twenty years. Indian trouble could not hold him from his duty, he and his wife knew. There had been intermittent fighting in the Connecticut Valley for two generations, and all the more reason that the folks needed religious help. His wife, who had given her name to Eunice, agreed completely with him, was willing to share all of the dangers of the frontier.

Young Eunice Williams slept without dreams that February 28 night. She felt both safe and warm. Her father was a veteran frontiersman who knew a great deal about Indians. Deerfield was protected by a stockade and fort. Soldiers were on guard all night long. Eunice snuggled deeper, pulled the pillow higher, and the blankets close about her neck.

Out across the smooth, snow-covered meadows, hidden among a grove of tall spruce, a force of fifty French soldiers and 200 Caughnawaga and Abenaki braves shivered while their commander counted off the minutes before attack would be right. He was Hertel de Rouville, a man still in his twenties and already a major in the Royal French Army and famous for his skill as a raider. Four of his brothers were with him tonight, and they like the rest crouched knee-down, their muskets held in mittened hands, their snowshoes off and stacked beside them.

Major de Rouville watched the village, and the loopholes of the fort. All of the lights were out in the houses with their small, narrow windows. But a fire had been built on the parade ground inside the stockade so the sentries could warm themselves. If the night was bitter enough to make Caughnawagas and Abenakis shiver, de Rouville knew, colonial militiamen would be tempted to stay near the fire and neglect their posts.

He rose to his feet and examined each loophole in turn. None was obscured by a human body; the firelight shone through to reflect in scarlet ripples on the snow. There were no sentries either on the catwalk of the stockade. The entire guard had gathered around the fire, possibly with a canteen of rum.

De Rouville wore Indian elkskin moccasins lined with rabbit fur, but beneath his cape the white silk uniform of his service and rank. He adjusted the brim of his black tricorne hat, as if about to go on parade. Then he touched the brace of pistols in his belt, threw off the cape and lifted his tomahawk. *"Allons-y,"* he told the men crouched beside him. "Let us go."

They ran at a lope over the hard-crusted snow, bent down low. But they were not fired upon; there was no challenge. They were at the stockade now, and de Rouville waved, and pointed. Warriors sprang up onto each other's shoulders and vaulted to the top of the stockade, and Frenchmen followed them. Then an Abenaki gave the warwhoop, and a scared militiaman screamed. A French musket banged. The man who screamed was struck by a tomahawk. The night was abruptly terrible.

Eunice Williams thought at first that this was a nightmare. She had gone through something like it before when she had eaten too much pumpkin pie. But the screaming continued, and the light came from the flames of burning houses. Those were really war-

whoops and musket shots; right here, in the doorway
of her room, her mother stood weeping and trying to
call to her. Behind her mother, much worse than any
nightmare figure, was an Abenaki warrior. His face
was painted green and yellow, with a band that
stretched from ear to ear. He wore rattlesnake skins
around his scalp lock, and his buckskins were splashed
with blood.

Eunice leaped sidewise from the bed. She tried to
pick up the chair on which her clothes lay. The
Abenaki had a long scalping knife at the center of her
mother's back. "No," her mother said very slowly; "no,
dear. 'Tis no use. They have all of us prisoners, even
father. Put on your clothes, before you freeze."

"Yes, mother," Eunice said dutifully, and yet she
was numb with shock. She did not need her mother to
tell her what had happened, and what went on at the
fort, and inside the houses which burned and where
the people were trapped. Her fingers fumbled at her
buttons and still she dressed warmly, with care. She
saw that her mother was fully dressed, although she
was white-faced and about to collapse. It was only a
few weeks ago that her mother had borne a new baby;
she wasn't too strong.

Eunice stepped forward and took her mother's hand
and the Abenaki growled like a wolf. But there was a

French officer beyond in the hall who talked with her father. He called some phrase the brave understood, for he stood back, then went down the stairs.

Reverend Williams came to the door of the room. He was still in his nightgown, his hands bound behind him. His face was without color, and the cheekbones were prominent. His big body was hunched, as though with pain. "I tried to fight," he said to Eunice. "But my pistol would not fire. Perhaps 'tis our good fortune. Else, they would have killed me, and all of us. Now we are safe."

"Safe from what, father?" Eunice said.

Reverend Williams indicated the French officer in the hall. "He has just promised to let me dress myself. I have given my word that I shall not attempt to fight against them. We are being taken to Canada as prisoners."

Eunice was too young to understand completely what her father had said. But she must have realized that for her family it meant great tragedy. Her mother sagged against the wall, hands caught together convulsively under her shawl. Downstairs and in the dooryard, she could hear her brothers and sisters, and some of them wept, and that was most unusual, particularly for the bigger boys.

The Williams family, the minister and his wife and

five of his children, were sent from Deerfield with the
rest of the captives an hour after dawn. Only one
strongly constructed and well-defended house still
resisted, tomahawks stuck in the door frame. Major
de Rouville had lost enough men and taken sufficient
plunder; he wanted to be on his way to Canada before
pursuit started. He gave the order for the remaining
houses to be set on fire, and the prisoners to be formed
into column.

There were 111 prisoners, and in the dawn, with the
flaming, gutted village as background, they were piti-
ful as they moved through the snow to the edge of the
forest. Forty of their neighbors had been killed. Here
in this column were sick women, and women who
carried small babies in their arms, and children just
able to walk, and men severely wounded in the fight-

ing. Before them was a march of at least 300 miles and of seven or eight weeks' duration. Half of their number were never to get home again to Deerfield.

Reverend Williams led the column, a pack filled with Indian plunder strapped to his back. He had several weeks ago asked his congregation to pass a day in fasting. Then he had preached a sermon whose text was, "Deliver me, I pray thee, from the hand of my brother, from the hand of Esau; for I fear him, lest he will come and smite me, and the mother with the children."

He could recognize the fatalities to come. There were no trails in the wilderness ahead. The weather would stay below zero all of the time. Neither the French nor the Indians had the habit of slowing a march for the wounded and sick.

Reverend Williams, looking around at his family, his friends, his neighbors, very likely gave himself to fervent prayer.

The column was halted at the edge of the forest and

Major de Rouville ordered the prisoners to take off their footgear. Some of the women wept in fright, but Reverend Williams understood, and explained to them. The Indians had brought along a supply of moccasins for the use of prisoners, and on the march through the wilderness English footgear would not last long.

Eunice was given a pair of moccasins that reached nearly kneehigh and that had porcupine quill designs on the sides. They were too big for her, but without a word an Abenaki brave stuffed the toes with dried moss he dug from underneath the snow. Eunice was overcome by admiration of them and by the way the French and Indians used toboggans and snowshoes.

Her mind would not accept any more tragedy. She had unconsciously raised a block against it. She was dully aware that three of her family were already dead, killed in last night's massacre, and that her mother was gravely ill. But she was by nature calm and happy, and she was physically strong. She strode forward in her file in the column and living from moment to moment, watched her moccasins slide through the snow.

De Rouville marched the column only four miles that day, made cooking fires before dusk and let the prisoners build shelters of pine boughs. Eunice slept close beside her mother, and held her mother's hand. But her sleep here was not like that at home. She was restless, and awake a good part of the time. She heard once a very faint, slow rustling, and almost spoke to her mother about it. Her mother was awake also, Eunice sensed, and had heard the sound.

Then Eunice understood. One of the captives, a Deerfield man, was escaping. Her mother placed her finger gently upon Eunice's lips. They lay absolutely still, even their breathing withdrawn. There was no shout of alarm, though, and after a while the rustling stopped as the man crawled away from the camp into the forest. The French and the Indians must be exhausted by their march from Canada and then the fighting at Deerfield, the girl realized, or they would not be so careless with their prisoners. Eunice squeezed her mother's hand and got a squeeze back. It was good to know that one of their own kind could escape.

The man was missed at dawn, though, and de Rouville came and talked sternly with Reverend Williams. He considered the minister to be the leader of the captive group, and if any more tried to escape, he told Williams, all of them would be burned at the stake. Williams could only nod and accept. There was no bargaining possible with the Frenchman.

Reverend Williams for part of the day walked be-

side his wife and supported her. Then he was sent
again to the head of the column and told to stay there.
Eunice could see his face as he passed her along the
files. It was gray with anguish, and haggard. Eunice
felt a sense of shock. Her father hardly looked like her
father any more.

The column was forced to ford the turbulent and icy
Green River that day. Reverend Williams struggled
through, his pack dragging at him, and was prodded
on up the steep hill beyond. Eunice watched him dis-
appear from sight, and was frightened. She would
drown in the river; she wasn't strong enough to cross
it. But a burly Caughnawaga brave swung her up in
his arms and splashed rapidly over, and some of her
brothers and sisters and other Deerfield children
hooted enviously at her. She looked back to see her
mother, and the brave grunted. That meant she should
sit still, Eunice sensed. She was already very weary,
and dozed in the man's arms.

She awoke when camp was made for the night and
the Caughnawaga in his greasy buckskins put her
down and left her. She sat quietly in the snow until
her father and her fifteen-year-old brother Samuel
came to her. Eunice was told by her father that her
mother was dead. Mrs. Williams had fallen while
crossing the Green River, risen and tried to keep on,

up the hill. Samuel had seen her there, and wanted to help her, and had been shoved along by the guards. Several Deerfield women had been with Mrs. Williams, though, at the end. They had refused to move until they had said prayers for her and arranged the body.

"Now let us pray," Reverend Williams said. His daughter and his son knelt beside him and further away in the camp, kept by chores the French had given them, the rest of the family stopped work and joined, and then all of the Deerfield people.

Eunice was never the same after that. Something went out of her with the news of her mother's death. She entered a sort of partial dream existence from which she only returned rarely to reality. The Caughnawaga brave who had befriended her must have sensed what had happened to her, and recognized that her mind was seized by demonic spirits from the nether world.

He made a carrying chair out of birchbark and buckskin straps for her. Then he put her on his back and carried her all of the way to Canada. It was a cruel march along the Connecticut River valley and the sharp, high spine of the Green Mountains, and across, to the Winooski, from the Winooski to frozen and wind-battered Lake Champlain, past the lake and into Canada.

Eunice emerged more and more from her vague, pleasant dreams as she became accustomed to the way she was carried and to the man who carried her. He was in her belief a giant, tireless, and marvelous. He

went up and down slopes without slipping, and sometimes she could reach out and pluck pine cones from
branches bent low by snow or ice, and nearly touch a
black squirrel that hunched red-eyed with fear on a
limb.

Her friend brought her bear meat to eat, and moose
meat, and berries, and ground nuts. She thanked him
several times, but he did not smile, and his expression
stayed the same. But this was not strange, she knew.
Other Indians had adopted prisoners with the consent
of the French. Her oldest sister, lame from the first day
of the march, was hauled by a brave on a toboggan. A
little Deerfield boy whose name she had forgotten but
who was familiar to her was now the pet of all the
Indians. When food was served out one night, he had
got none, and had gone straight across the camp to
an old Abenaki warrior. He snatched away the marrow
bone on which the Abenaki chewed, and began to
chew on it himself. Reverend Williams sprang up to
protect the boy, and then the warrior laughed. The
Abenaki took the boy in his arms, kept him warm
under his blanket, and explained by sign language
that he was to be his adopted son.

So not all Indians were bad, Eunice realized. And
some were very good. She still prayed whenever her
father asked her, and sang hymns along with the other

Deerfield people. But she no longer felt much like a Christian. She was very eager to see Canada, and how the Indians lived.

The column, slow, weary, skidding along the Richelieu River ice past Lake Champlain, came after twenty-five days to Chambly. It was a fortified town below Montreal, and here the prisoners were separated. Eunice was taken alone to a place called Mission St. Louis which had the Indian name of Caughnawaga. Her father protested. He was afraid for her future, under the influence of Jesuit priests, and among Indians. But he was lucky to be allowed to go on by canoe the fifteen miles from Chambly to Montreal and meet the governor, de Vaudrel, and appeal to him.

Governor de Vaudrel and his wife were impressed by the gaunt Protestant minister. They believed he had every right to claim Eunice and keep her with him until he could arrange for their ransom and that of the rest of his family. De Vaudrel appealed personally to the Jesuits at Mission St. Louis. He offered an Indian girl to replace Eunice, and the sum of 100 louis d'or. His offers were refused, and those his wife made. The Jesuits said that Reverend Williams could only see his daughter for an hour, no more.

Reverend Williams went to Mission St. Louis by canoe. He climbed ashore and walked past the slab-

walled cabins occupied by the Caughnawagas who
had become Catholics and worshipped in the chapel
at the end of the street. A Jesuit in black habit met him
at the gateway of the mission, took him in quietly and
led him to Eunice.

His daughter sat quite prim in new French clothing,
her hands folded in her lap. She rose and kissed his

cheek, but she did not cry or show much emotion when
he told her that he could only stay for an hour. They
talked about the past, and Deerfield, and the other
English children who were here at the mission. Then
it was time for Reverend Williams to go. He kissed
Eunice again, and she promised him not to forget her
catechism. The Jesuit was waiting at the door, and
there was no more to be said.

Eunice stayed at Mission St. Louis for over two

years. She became a Catholic, and made her life in Canada. When she was still in her early teens, in regular frontier style, she was married. Her husband was a Caughnawaga brave. The record does not tell much about him except that he chose to take Eunice's family name of Williams, and that Eunice lived happily with him, and bore him many children.

Reverend Williams remained in Canada until October 25, 1706, when he left Quebec for Boston. He had been able to arrange for the freedom of four of his children and to send them home. Three of his sons went to Harvard, and one, Stephen, who had made the frightful march, became a minister and took a pulpit in Deerfield, where Reverend Williams had returned to preach.

But Eunice did not stay away from Deerfield. She came back to it first in 1740, with her Caughnawaga husband and her half-breed children. They followed the traditional raiders' route, down Lake Champlain and the Winooski River to the Connecticut. They arrived in sumertime, and they were welcomed by the Williams family.

Eunice was a "blanket squaw," and the women in Deerfield persuaded her to put on a dress when she went to church. She wore it only once, although she and her husband and their children returned several more times to the village.

They made the journey always in summer, while they could pick berries, and catch fish in the streams and ponds and lakes. Perhaps, only remembering a little of it now, Eunice told her sons and daughters of the original march she had made. She might have explained to them why she had come to love and marry an Indian, and the meaning of forgiveness.

MAINE TOOK the worst of the Indian warfare right from the beginning to the end, when in 1759, finally, Wolfe captured Quebec. A peculiar breed of people was needed to live in Maine, and John Gyles and his family belonged to it. They farmed land they had cleared themselves at Point Pleasant, on Merrymeeting Bay.

John never doubted for a moment that whites were entitled to all of the rich and beautiful land north of the Merrimac. Indians simply did not count; they were a lazy lot, lacking brains and an understanding of the uses of the soil. The tribes should get out, go to Canada, go somewhere else.

So John became an Indian hater, and a superb border fighter. Little is known about him. The settlements were burned time and again, and with them the records. We are lucky to have the name of John's father, although the name of the brother who was burned at the stake at Castine has not come down to us.

The spare, broken record must be amplified by surmise and what might logically have happened under the circumstances. He was all too real to the Abenakis, though, and he served for some years in Brunswick and other parts of Maine after he returned from captivity in Canada.

His kind has been well-described by Robert P. Tristram Coffin, the Maine historian:

"The people who were still alive at the close of the Indian wars were tough people. They could live through anything. The coming Revolution would be a mere picnic. They had been tried by the snows of Maine winters, by ice and hunger. They had been tried by the Indians. They had been rocked in a cradle of fire."

Chapter 6

BLOODY MAINE

It was the sudden instant of silence that warned the boy. All the summer morning became still: the birds and squirrels at the edge of the forest, the crows that had been cawing busily above the cleared land around the cabin, even a fish hawk out over the beach and ducks in the backwater. Then John Gyles knew, and started to run for the cabin. The old musket was propped just inside the door.

Looking back over his shoulder as he ran, not slowing down and running faster, he saw the Abenaki braves at the edge of the forest and his father and the two hired men where they worked pulling stumps. His father was already trapped, John saw; Thomas Gyles had been caught yards away from his musket. Thomas Gyles shouted when the tomahawks flashed, and told the hired men to fire their muskets. The braves killed him, though, and then the hired men, right there in the clearing.

John Gyles reached the cabin. He picked up the old English musket. It was already loaded and primed. He braced himself against the door frame and shot between the shoulders the Abenaki who had scalped his father. Then he was aware that his mother, his younger brother and the other, smaller children were behind him in the cabin, crouched down in fear, wordless and motionless. John was in his early teens, and this was 1755 and the coast of Maine. He called harsh defiance at the Abenakis and their French officer and began to reload the musket.

Big, stinking, painted warriors stopped him. They plunged through the doorway and seized him, knocked down the musket. He was almost unconscious with pain, only saw the scalping knife very dimly when he heard the French officer tell the brave who held him to let him go. "No," the Frenchman said. "We will keep them to sell. The woman, the two boys, the small children. You will get rum. Rum and tobacco."

The warrior made a deep-throated sound and dropped John to the floor. His hair had been yanked so hard his head throbbed, and alongside him his mother softly wept. She clasped his younger brother in her arms and tried to hide the smaller children beneath her skirts. It was all right for her to do that, John admitted to himself. His father's first wife had been killed outside here some years ago, scalped while she worked in the garden.

Now they were all of the Gyles family left. And from what he could understand of the French officer's talk to the Abenakis, they were bound for Canada and the long, terrible march into slavery.

The Gyles farm was on Point Pleasant at Merry-meeting Bay, below Brunswick. The calm, windless air bore many tall columns of smoke from the homes of neighbors. A musket volley slapped once, and there were single shots, and John thought that several times he heard screams.

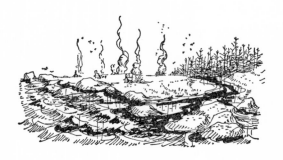

But his own home was being burned. He watched at first with wild rage, and then quietly, deep down, he made a promise to himself to pay back, and get vengeance for this. Embers from the chimney-place fire had been scattered across the cabin floor, and braves tossed in armloads of dry marsh hay that spurted with yellow flame. The cabin walls and roof were of pine; they burned fast.

John watched, and heard his mother's weeping. A brave slit the throat of the tethered cow with a scalping knife. Brands from the cabin were flung in the sheds; even the bottom of his father's canoe on the beach was knocked out by hatchet blows. Then, as the Frenchman started to gather the party together and ordered the braves to leave, they shot arrows at the family dog.

John's brother cursed the braves for it. He yelled insults at them in broken Abenaki phrases. A brave stopped him with a clout on the ear and whacked him flat. John helped his brother up and whispered to him to be still. They could not win here. But his brother remained furious. He told John that John was a coward for not talking up against the dog being killed. Then the French officer pointed to the Abenaki canoes hidden further on along the beach, and there was no more time to talk.

The raiding party went up the Androscoggin River with the prisoners. The Abenakis wanted to take advantage of their canoes as long as they could, John realized. He studied these men intently, marking the way they paddled, made portages and night camps, hunted briefly for game or fished the river. They were his enemies, he told himself; he would give all of his life to fighting them. He hated the French officer, too, but not for the same reasons, and not as much. The French in themselves were no real threat to the Maine people.

It was the Indians who refused to let the whites have the Maine land. The tribes were so lazy, so careless as farmers and fishermen, that each warrior needed at least fifty acres for his hunting, and a white man could keep himself and his family on what he raised on one. So the Indians raided, looted, scalped and burned, thought they could scare the Maine folk out of the country. Not John Gyles.

John controlled himself, held his temper. The party moved alone, and yet along the river they found signs of where other raiders had passed with captives. A small wooden doll that had yellow hemp hair was seen bobbing and tossing in the river eddies one day. Near a shelving beach, among windfall timber, wolves stared up slant-eyed as they pulled at the bones of a cadaver. Tatters of a woman's skirt hung from the

windfall branches. John's mother screamed, her hands over her mouth.

John's younger brother escaped that night. He whispered to John that he was going to make a try for the coast before it was too far away. It was too far away now, John told him. His brother could never outrun the braves in the forest; he was certain to be caught. Stay, and wait for a better chance in Canada, and then they would escape together. John's brother was silent. He still secretly believed that John was a coward, John knew.

The brother got away into the forest before dawn. The Frenchman found out at dawn and sent a single warrior after him. Then the party moved on towards Canada.

The brave was back in three weeks. He rejoined at a night camp site near Dixville Notch in the high, rugged White Mountains country. The man's moccasins were badly worn, John saw, but the warrior wore fresh war paint and carried a fresh scalp at his belt. He leaned forward to tell the French officer how the boy had died at the stake in Castine, on the coast. That scalp had belonged to his brother, John realized. He turned away, sick at heart, and then noticed his mother. She lay as though dead, only her sobs slightly shaking her shoulders.

The party marched steadily through the mountainous country. It crossed the Connecticut River below
Beechers Falls, and went past Lake Memphremagog,
holding to the north for the St. Francis and the first
Canadian settlement. That was St. Francis, on the
river of the same name, and hundreds of scalps hung
from poles in the miserable slab-cabin village al-

though it contained a church and the Indians who
lived there were suposed to have been converted to
Christianity.

John Gyles studied the settlement just as he had all
of the country between it and Merrymeeting Bay. His
resolve was very clear in his mind. No matter how long
he might be forced to stay in Canada, he would finally
go home, take vengeance upon the Indians then or
later.

The Gyles family survivors were separated at

Chambly, a fortified trading post and town fifteen miles below Montreal on the Richelieu River. It is very probable that they never met John again, although there is no record of what happened to them. The French and their Indian allies who bought the English captives sent them far, and a husky young

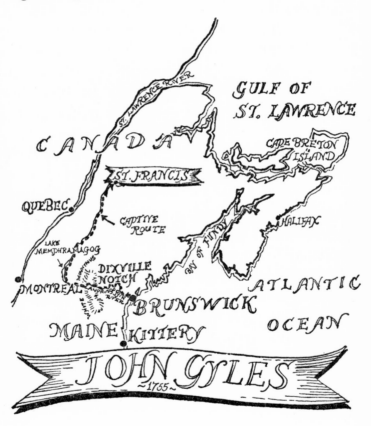

teen-ager like John must have seen a great deal of eastern and central Canada.

He was a captive for eight years, and in that time he learned a great deal. He discovered that the French treated the Indians as human beings, something his own people had never done. The French intermarried with the tribes, took on many of their ways and habits, and the Jesuits were fearless, boundless in their energy, went into wholly wild and unknown regions after converts. The French also did not destroy the forest in the wholesale fashion of the English. They kept a major part intact so that they might procure furs.

It became easier for John to understand why he saw at the various French posts where he worked as a slave laborer so many Maine Indians. He saw Norridgewock braves from the Kennebec, Penobscots and Androscoggins, Pennacooks from the Merrimac and Pequawkets from the Saco. They were all "praying Indians," Catholic converts, but they walked with a freedom, a dignity they could not show in an English colonial village.

Along with his knowledge of the Indians, he picked up a vast amount of information about the French. There would be a day, he knew, when he would use all this. The French still handled the northern tribes pretty much as they wished, and could destroy the

Maine settlements almost at will. Here in Canada, the Royal Governor appointed by the King in Paris maintained a very rigid system.

Men called *grand seigneurs* either ruled or owned huge regions under the authority of the Governor General. Below the *seigneurs* on the scale were men called *bourgeois,* or *fermiers,* who were usually former army officers. They carried a *fermé*—a permit to trade with the Indians, and there were several hundred of them who lived at distant posts in the interior.

John Gyles envied them their lives although he was forever homesick for Maine and Merrymeeting Bay. The French traders were in command of thousands of carefree, wild and yet canny and extremely brave *coureurs de bois* and *voyageurs* who gathered furs from the Indians.

Those men roamed the wilderness on voyages that lasted about a year but sometimes were as long as two and three years. They sailed the rivers and lakes to the south and west of Montreal in the birchbark, resin-sealed canoes they had made famous. *Voyageurs* had reached the fabulous lakes that were like inland seas, and held barter with the Assiniboins, the Sioux, the Miamis and the Illinois. When they returned to Montreal, their buckskins blackened, their hair, their beards matted with mosquitoes, flies and bear grease,

Iroquois scalps at their belts, they caroused for a month straight after they had sold their furs for immense profit. People stayed out of the Lower Town taverns while the *voyageurs* drank themselves back into poverty.

John Gyles had no deep interest in Canada, though, that matched his love of Maine. His homesickness became acute after eight years of captivity, and he planned in thorough detail the fashion in which he would escape. He chose to go in wintertime, when chance of pursuit was less, and to travel alone, so that he could follow a raiding party headed for the Maine coastal settlements.

His plan was both daring and extremely ingenious. It was about the only one a single person, poorly armed and without extra food, could use and hope to survive. John Gyles had calculated all of the danger. He might well be captured, and after torture burned at the stake, or freeze to death in the snow, starve, be caught by wolves. Still, he was going to make a try to get home.

He waited until a party of about forty braves and French provincial troops left for a raid on Maine. They made no secret of their departure, and once he was away from the Richelieu River farmhouse where he had lived as a laborer, John had no trouble following them. But he was forced to wait for darkness, and it was piercingly cold. His homespun clothing and blanket coat were old, thin, and the snowshoes he had stolen and hidden were warped. He carried no food except a pig's bladder filled with cornmeal. His weapon was a broken-bladed skinning knife.

Near dawn of that first night he nearly caught up to the party, and then stayed in their broad, meshed track to throw off pursuit. They kept on down the Richelieu River to Lake Champlain, and marching fast, crossed it to the Winooski River valley. He had eaten almost the entire content of the pig's bladder by that time, and was famished. But he believed that pretty soon the party would start to hunt for game, cache some of it for rations to supply them on the return march.

He heard distant musket shots during the next day, and marked the smoke of a hardwood fire, smelled roasting meat on the wind. He waited, part-crazy with hunger, and after dusk, moving along the hunters' track, came to where a haunch of what had been a brown bear was buried in thick snow. He ate all he could of the meat, made a package with birchbark strips of some of the rest, left what remained for the wolves, the wolverines, the lynx, cougars and crows.

His work after that as the party headed east through the forests that led to the English settlements was quite systematic. He destroyed each meat cache that was deposited as return march rations. The party would count on these, he knew, and various Abenaki warriors and scalp-carrying Frenchmen might well starve to death because of their loss.

John Gyles ate what he wanted, of bear and moose and elk and deer meat, and of partridge and squirrel. What he did not need and could not take along until he found the next cache, he destroyed. Then the party emerged from the last of the White Mountain slopes and was on the headwaters of the Saco River. John hurried to catch up with it. He would be leaving here and turning off on his own for Merrymeeting Bay.

The French officer in command of the raiders was an efficient soldier. He kept a big Abenaki brave in a black squirrel cloak and knee-high moccasins back about a hundred yards as rear-guard. John moved soundlessly in the snow on the river ice. He killed the Abenaki with a blow in the throat from the skinning knife as the warrior turned, having smelled or sensed him, and about to shout.

John did not take the scalp, although he thought of his brother, his father, his father's first wife and all the rest. He was content with the cloak and the fine pair of snowshoes, the musket of English manufacture, the powder horn and shotbag. Then he went swiftly running into the forest on the snowshoes, did not stop until night, when he knew pursuit was impossible.

He was safe with dawn, and took his own time to reach Point Pleasant and the bay. Most of the old neighbors were dead, or had been replaced by new.

But enough recognized him to give him a real welcome. He was happy to be back, he said.

John Gyles was made captain of the nearby Brunswick fort soon after he was home. That pleased him
more than the welcome. He could help defend Maine.
It would belong to him and folks like him for a long
time.

JOHN MILLEDGE shared the sense of independence that was cherished so much by John Gyles. Still, this other John, in the new colony of Georgia in the middle 1730's, was somewhat different in his attitude. The Indian problem was not at all as serious, and the major difficulty for John Milledge was that the professional do-gooders would not let him and his orphaned family of younger children take care of themselves.

John Milledge hated poverty and anything that had to do with the poor-house just as much as John Gyles hated Abenakis. The colony had been founded in good part to give support to paupers and people released from debtors' prison in England. But John Milledge's family was not among them, and John, young, hard-worked, perplexed, was determined that none of his folks would ever be.

His son, still another John, followed along in his beliefs, became a more famous citizen of Georgia, but in no way a better man.

Chapter 7

JOHN MILLEDGE'S PRIDE

Alligators lay in the mud and made snuffling and barking noises as the boat crossed the river. John Milledge sat quite still on the thwart and looked from the alligators at the Indians up above on the bluff. He was eleven years old, and frightened, and willing to admit it to anybody who asked him. But, he noticed, his father and mother kept very quiet, and his brothers and sisters, younger than he, were openly awed, if not scared stiff.

The boat reached the bank. James Edward Oglethorpe, governor of the new Georgia colony, jumped ashore, and Colonel William Bull from Charles Town, South Carolina, sprang after him. The two men began to climb up the steep slope of the bluff, moving slowly in their long boots, their swords tipped high to clear the scrub brush. Among the pines at the top of the bluff, the Indians stood motionless yet, bizarre and barbaric figures to the people in the boat.

Then from the ship, the *Ann,* which had brought the group of 112 colonists from England, a small brass cannon rapped a report over the Savannah River. This was February 12, 1773, and the captain of the ship, once he had his anchor down, considered it an historic moment. The cannon was fired in salute, and also to awe the Indians.

Governor Oglethorpe had just met the old Yamacraw chief, Tomochichi. He stood flanked by Colonel Bull and the Indian trader and interpreter, John Musgrove, when the Milledge family struggled up the slope from the boat. Young John Milledge had lost a lot of his fright, and he moved away from his father and mother, started to investigate on his own. He stood for a while and listened to the conversation between the English officers and Tomochichi, barely understanding it, although Mary Musgrove, the interpreter's half-breed wife, repeated many of the phrases in both languages.

John Milledge was more interested in the fact that the Indians were straight, fine-looking people and that very few of the men wore anything except a breech-clout. But Tomochichi and the other senior warriors wore cloaks of coarse-woven hemp, and loose drawers, and pieces of cloth wrapped around their legs in puttee fashion. The women wore calico jackets and skirts, and John realized that they must have bartered for the material over in Charles Town, where many Indians went to trade, and where his ship had first touched on her way from England.

He wandered on through the pine grove, sharply sniffing the scent of turpentine sap. Skinny, short-haired Indian dogs yapped at him, and Indian boys glared as he came near their village. He was abruptly conscious that he was very pale and small alongside these boys, and strangely dressed in his tight knee pants, stockings and thick-soled shoes. The Indian boys went barefoot, and soon he would, too, he promised himself.

He left the village with its huts built of bark and saplings and looked for his family. It was wrong for him to have been gone so long. His father counted on him a great deal for help. He was the eldest of the children here, and while Richard was eight, and Sarah about a year younger, and they could be useful, there were Frances, who was five, and James, just over a year and a half and still tumbling and a constant care for his mother.

John found his father busy with a measuring rod and a hatchet at the edge of the grove. Thomas Milledge was forty-two when the colonists landed, and his wife

Elizabeth was forty. They had left England eagerly to make their life in the new colony. Milledge was a highly skilled carpenter and joiner, and Governor Oglethorpe had great respect for his ability. Now Milledge laid out the site where he would build his cabin, and temporarily put up a shelter of saplings covered by ship tarpaulins.

He sent John to bring the needed tarpaulins from the *Ann,* and told him that Oglethorpe had entered into a treaty with Tomochichi. The Yamacraws were a small outlaw band that really belonged to the Lower Creek tribe, and had only settled here in 1730, and Tomochichi was the chief of no more than a hundred people who made up seventeen or eighteen families. The chief was glad to have dealings with the English. It gave him the chance for barter and protection against the other Creeks who did not like the fact that he had left the tribe.

John was very busy during the next few days while he worked beside his father and they built the slab-walled cabin and put up a chimney made of clay and sticks. The nights were cold and a fire was needed. John was pleased to wake up in the dawn light and see the embers cherry-red in the chimney place, take a long stretch on his pine bough pallet before he got up and put on fresh logs. Then he went to the river for water.

He carried the water in a pair of wooden buckets his father had fashioned, and bore them on a yoke over his shoulder. The Indian boys he met down at the river

were curious about the yoke and how his father had made the buckets. Their own were made out of birch bark sealed with pine resin, but they did not have many of them and they explained by sign language that birches did not grow locally, and the bark had been brought from inland.

John found that every day he could understand a little more of the Creek sign language. He began to answer the boys in it, and to identify game and fish and birds with Indian words he had learned. There were tall red deer with big racks off in the forest, and turkey buzzards and partridge and many kinds of smaller birds. The river held small, sweet shrimp, and oysters, and sturgeon, trout, perch, catfish and rockfish. Across the river, in the flatlands where broom grass and wild rice grew were tern and snipe and blue wing teal, shoveller and ring neck ducks.

John's father had brought a matchlock musket from England, and after the cabin was built he and John went hunting. They crossed the river in a dugout canoe borrowed from a Yamacraw brave and went out into the flatland. Thomas Milledge loaded the match-

lock with bird shot and let John carry the powder horn and shot bag. They moved quietly through the broom grass to the edge of a slough where palmettos and syca-mores and willows grew, the bigger trees hung with tattered yellow streamers of Spanish moss. A wild turkey went sqwonking up from the slough, a pair of terns right behind him, and John's father got the turkey and a tern with a single shot.

John was quick to praise him, but his father only shook his head. He said, " 'Tis a pity I haven't a dog such as in England. But this is not the country for it. The snakes would kill the beast, or one of those monster alligators. Go fetch the fowl, John."

"Gladly," John said, and went off at a lope into the slough.

But there was not often a chance for him to go hunting with his father. There was a tremendous amount of work for Thomas Milledge to do in the new village. Governor Oglethorpe was ambitious and hard-driving, determined to carry out all of the requests of the colony's board of trustees. John found out from his father and mother that there were twenty trustees who by their own regulations could not occupy any other office or hold land in the colony.

The colony had been founded for several reasons, to take care of poor people and those who were in debtors' prison, to settle in territory that might otherwise be claimed by the Spanish, and to establish a source of supply for the Royal Navy and a base for the Army. More than that, in an immediate fashion, the colonists were supposed to make silk, wine and various tropical and semi-tropical products for the English and European markets.

Every adult male in the colony who was able to fight in the case of Spanish or Indian attack was given fifty acres of land. The people who had paid for their passage from England were entitled to 500 acres of land. But according to the trustees each colonist was to plant 100 white mulberry trees to start silk manufacture, and also raise grapes and cultivate gardens.

The plans did not come out exactly as they had been created in London. A number of the men found they could make more money for themselves cutting timber and raising cattle than by farming. They traded over in Charles Town or with the ship captains who navigated the tortuous windings of the Savannah River up from the sea. Rum had been forbidden in the colony because the trustees believed it to be a great source of harm. It was commonly drunk, though, and Oglethorpe could not stop the use of it.

He had already allowed that every man have a pint of strong beer each night after work, and "other frequent Refreshments." He wrote this in his journal along with the fact that the people had put down gardens and were raising plenty of Indian corn although the extreme summer heat, the sand flies and the half-inch long ants had begun to bother them a great deal. Still, Oglethorpe wrote, they cultivated "Thyme, with other sorts of Pot-herbs, Sage, Leeks, Skellions, Celeri, Liquorice &c and several sorts of Fruit-trees."

Oglethorpe had become a good friend of Tomochichi, and the Yamacraw chief saw that his braves sold venison at a cheap price to the settlers. The people were issued by agreement with the trustees a basic diet of meat and flour, and the annual ration was fifteen bushels of Indian corn, a barrel of beef, 64 quarts of molasses, and twelve gallons of lamp oil and a pound of spun cotton for lamp wicking.

Oglethorpe put in the record that the ants bit "desperately" and "Camphire" helped fly stings, and people had begun to build up a partial immunity. An alligator that had strayed up the bluff from the river was seen and shot, the carcass given to the Indian dogs. But there was no protection against mosquitoes, and the water everybody drank came from the muddy, sluggish Savannah. Malaria began to kill, and kept on until in the first summer forty settlers were dead.

Others staggered around slack-kneed and skeletal, and many more, whom Oglethorpe bitterly called the "Grumbletonians" talked only of going home. They mocked him and openly dared him to put them in the stocks, the pillory or the village jail. He took no action against them, aware that a ship would arrive soon from England and then his position would be greatly strengthened. The Grumbletonians were to end up being heavily fined, or sent to England in irons. Meantime, life in the colony must go on despite the terrible fever toll.

John Milledge felt some of the governor's intense worry. He had made a close friend of Toonahawi, a very bright Yamacraw boy. Toonahawi was the adopted son of the chief, and his father was pleased to have him spend his time with the whites. Toonahawi had learned to speak, read and write English, and to calculate mathematical sums. He explained to John that the Indians protected themselves against mosquitoes by smearing their bodies with bear grease. Still, a number of them were caught by the fever, and those who survived never again got it.

John thanked his friend and took from him a bowl filled with bear grease. But when he brought it home and talked with his father and mother they shrugged and said that to use the stuff was nothing but a stupid, nasty Indian trick. It would only attract more mosquitoes, or the ants.

John did not have any answer. His tall father lay in the bed gaunt and yellow-skinned and gasping. The fever shook him so that his teeth rattled, and his sweat made a pool under the bed. John had seen other strong men die like this during the spring and summer. He knew that his father was about to die, and that his mother, pregnant and about to bear a baby, was also very ill.

A sense of panic seized him, and he wondered for just a moment what he would do if both his parents were to die. Then he took control of himself, quietly gathered together his younger brothers and sisters, cooked supper for them and his mother. His mother sat limp against the wall and slowly stroked his hair. She told him that he was a good boy, her pride, and that she dearly loved him. John was embarrassed. He was just big enough to dislike any expression of affection. It was a relief for him when a messenger from Governor Oglethorpe came across the clearing to the cabin.

There was to be a meeting of the first jury of freeholders in the colony, the messenger told John. He had been sent to summon John to sit as a member. So many men were ill of the fever, or dead, that some of their sons must be called. John nodded to his mother, took another look in at his father, and asked his sisters and brothers to be good while he was gone. Then he went with the messenger to the meeting-house.

Sam Parker was among those called for jury duty,

John Milledge saw, and said hello to the other boy. Sam was sixteen, and his father had just died of the fever. So he was here to serve. John walked in beside him, and calmly, conscious that he was not yet twelve years old and occupied his father's place, gave his name to the clerk of the court. Then the jury was empanelled and he was made a member, was assigned to service along with Sam.

He went home after jury duty to find that his father was nearly dead. There was nothing to be done but bathe the emaciated face, hold the twisted body as the fever shook it. Thomas Milledge died July 29, 1733. His wife gave birth on August 9 and lay sick and helpless for weeks. John took care of the family.

He prepared his father for burial with the help of neighbor women, accompanied the body to the graveyard. When he returned home, the neighbor women asked if they might help him more. But he knew that despite aid from anybody he must now take his father's place. He was the head of the Milledge family, and should start acting like it right away.

His mother, although she recouped her strength a bit after her husband's death, remained weak and unable to do much around the house. John did most of the simple cooking, tended the family garden and kept track of his brood of brothers and sisters. Then he was given assistance by the trustees, who according to the regulations of the colony assigned an indentured servant to each widow, and supplied enough bricks for a chimney. The South Carolina folks helped further by sending each Savannah family a milch cow.

John worked hard with the servant, a hulking big Irishman, and tore down the old stick and clay chimney, laid up a stack of the fine, smooth brick carried as ship ballast from England. He learned to milk the cow and keep the cow's tail out of his face, her hooves out of the bucket. But the Irishman died from fever a month after he had been assigned to the Milledge family, and the cow developed the habit that had been disastrous to so many others and ran away into the woods, where stray Indians and wolves found an easy meal.

John was given a break from the galling routine of his life when the 138-ton London ship *Georgia Pink* came up the river and went to anchor opposite the bluff in late August. He put his hoe aside in the corn patch rows, and with Richard and Sarah and Frances and James, because they were excited, too, went to watch the ship discharge her cargo. She held a marvellous assortment, John learned: cannon, and muskets, and powder and ball, swords, vinegar, beer, fresh water in casks, oatmeal, bedding, tarpaulins for tents, drugs, nails, knives, hatchets, and lucerne seed. There were copies of *The Great Importance of a Religious Life Considered*, and *The Duty of Man*, and *Friendly Admonitions to the Drinkers of Brandy*.

The young Milledges were not as impressed by the cargo, though, as they were by the passengers. *Georgia Pink* had carried upholsterers and tailors, peruke-makers and shoe-makers, a sawmill wright, and an ale-house keeper, and shopkeepers, and a hatter, a silver-smith and a bookseller. John knew from talk he had heard at Thomas Causton's store, until now the only one in the colony, that Savannah would not stay a small settlement long with the arrival of these people.

John Musgrove and Thomas Wiggan, the Indian traders, were already worried about the effect on the Creeks of the loss of more of their hunting grounds. John Milledge in his turn gave serious thought about what might happen to his family's property. Title to it was not too clear after the death of his father.

He went to have a talk with Governor Oglethorpe.

The governor was a great admirer of the lean, whip-cord-hard boy, and he sat on his porch and swatted away flies and patiently listened to him. His advice was that John go to England and make a direct appeal for a settlement of the title to the property before the Common Council of the trustees of the colony. Oglethorpe himself was leaving on the next ship and taking a party of warriors under Tomochichi for a London visit. He would arrange for John to go along, and see that his lodging and expenses were paid while he was in England.

John, deeply pleased and grateful, went running home to tell his mother. She lay very still, and John knew that she was gripped by grief because her baby had died. She seemed to hear no more than half of what John said.

But she managed to tell John clearly that in England he had an older brother, Thomas, and a sister, Mary, who had been left there when the rest of the family came out to Georgia. From what little she knew of the law, John's mother said, his brother Thomas would inherit the property. Then she was silent, her strength gone, and outside the summer rain drubbed, bouncing in a splatter from the red clay soil of the dooryard. John knelt at the hearth and started supper before the fire might be doused by rain down the chimney.

It would be fine to get to England, he thought. He should put things straight, and lose some of this gnawing worry that was always in the back of his head. Toonahawi and his other good friend, Sam Parker, had asked him a number of times recently, had he forgotten how to smile? Maybe he would pick up the habit again aboard ship, or in London when he met his brother Thomas, his sister Mary.

John sailed aboard Governor Oglethorpe's ship in the summer of 1734 and on October 7 he appeared before the Common Council of the trustees in London. But there had been further tragedy at home; on June 2, during one of the drenching, protracted rains, his mother had died. John was a sober-faced, gaunt boy when he stood in his homespun clothing in the great hall of the Council and answered to his name.

Governor Oglethorpe had already spoken in his behalf, and the members of the Council were well-disposed towards John. They listened to his plea for a clearance of the property title, and to the sworn statement that his brother Thomas had given his permission to bring about the transfer. The members in their elaborate wigs and high stocks and cravats consulted gravely with each other, then a decision was given. They ordered that Thomas Milledge, son of Thomas Milledge, deceased, might have license to lease his house and lot to his brother John Milledge, so "that he may be enabled to take care of his two Sisters and Younger Brothers in Georgia."

John stood and bowed to the members after the decision was sonorously read by the clerk of the Council. Then the clerk inhaled and read an addition to it: John Milledge was to have his passage home paid by the council of trustees, and he was to be given an indentured servant. More: "John Milledge must be look'd on as a Freeman, and must not be apprenticed out to any other person."

Thirteen-year-old John was very probably close to tears of surprised gratitude while he stood there in the somber, ornate hall. This was most unusual procedure. He had just been accorded incredibly generous treatment, a minor, a poor boy, and an orphan. It was all he could do to bow again to the members, and to Governor Oglethorpe, and make his way out into the anteroom where his brother Thomas and his sister Mary waited for him.

He had several times during his stay in London impressed them with his stories of alligators, Indians and wolves, and he had taken them to meet Tomochichi and the other Yamacraw braves. Now he found that they were impressed in a far more profound fashion, and they walked beside him in the street with unconcealed admiration in their glances.

John sailed for Georgia again aboard the *Prince of Wales* on October 31, 1734, and took along his assigned servant, John Shears. The ship left from Gravesend and her master, George Dunbar, was happy to have John stand at his side while she hauled her wind and cleared for the Channel. There was a rather odd company this voyage, Captain Dunbar told John. Beside Tomochichi and the rest of the Yamacraws, dazed by their London experience, there were 57 Salzburgers being sent out as colonists, and twenty-two English folk. Christmas would certainly be celebrated at sea, and should prove quite an occasion.

John enjoyed himself greatly at Christmas, and saw that John Shears received a fair part of all food and drink. He was grateful to the trustees for the servant, but he had been too close to servitude himself to think much of indenture. He planned as soon as possible to give Shears his freedom and let the man go on his own.

Prince of Wales made a fifty-day passage from Gravesend to Savannah, anchored off the Yamacraw bluff with a weary company aboard. John and his servant were among the first ashore, and on the bank his family met him. But little Jamie, the smallest, was missing, John saw. His two sisters, Sarah and Frances, and his remaining brother, Richard, told him of Jamie's death while they stood close, their arms around him.

He walked up the familiar bluff bewildered and saddened. It seemed now that all the effort spent in London was wasted. He was too young yet to play both father and mother to this lot. They needed older folks to tend to them, and the colony had already established a plan to care for orphans. Four of the "Best Persons" were supposed to handle them, make sure they received the right treatment. But, when he started to speak to his brother and sisters about it, the girls cried, and all of them asked him to try it on his own.

John did. His love for them was just that much, and his ability. Edward Jenkins, one of the colonists whose duty was to supervise orphans, checked on John soon after John's return from England. He maintained a watch on him and in 1735 he reported in writing to the trustees: "John Milledge have put him up a hut by ye help of Mr. Young and some of his Neighbours. He desired we would let his Brother and sisters live with him as we have Consented to. But I fear its two (sic) young a family to do well. If they do not we will part ym."

John, though, and his brothers and sisters were getting along fine. Mr. Young was Thomas Young, a friend of his father, who had come out in the *Ann* with the family. He and other neighbors helped John build the hut because John could rent the Milledge house. When the hut was finished, the children moved in, and John rented the house to a man named Robert Parker for fourteen pounds a year.

Governor Oglethorpe was back in the colony from England, and he kept an eye on John's activities. He learned that John's servant had drowned, so he found another, named John Stout. Oglethorpe called John in to inform him, and to ask if he would like to take charge of some oxen owned by trustees and haul timber for the colony. John said that he was pleased, and once more grateful. He took the new servant and the span of oxen, put his brother and sisters in the care of reliable neighbors and went into the forest to the section where the timber was to be cut.

He was busy in the forest felling and trimming trees and snaking logs over a skidroad when a famous English evangelist, George Whitefield returned to Savannah for a second time. This was on January 11, 1740, and Whitefield was completely convinced that the colony needed an orphan asylum. He rented the David Douglass house for the purpose as soon as he was ashore from his sloop. Then, January 19, short of orphans to put in the place, he seized John's brother Richard, who was thirteen, and his sister Frances, who was twelve.

It was done despite the protests of their neighbors, and when Oglethorpe was informed, he wrote a formal objection:

"As for Milledge's brother and Sister I think yr. representation is very just, that the taking them away to the Orphan House will break up a family, which is in a way living comfortably. Mr. Whitefield's design is for the good of ye people and the Glory of God, and I dare say, when he considers this he will be very well satisfied with the Boy and Girl's returning: to their Brother John Milledge, since they can assist him, and you may allow them upon my account the Provisions they used to have upon the Orphanage account."

John came in from the skidroad, talked with Governor Oglethorpe, and on March 25 went to see Whitefield. The hot-eyed evangelist told him that his brother and sister were already at their proper home. Whitefield knew of no other home to which they might go. Then he said to John, "You can tell General Oglethorpe I said so."

John was big for his age now, and his hands were lumpy with axe helve and saw handle callouses. He could, he knew, pick up this man and heave him through the orphanage window. But it would do his brother and sister little good, and eventually get Governor Oglethorpe in trouble. He had learned the value of patience some time ago, and here was the place to use a bit. "Yes, sir," he said, and made a very small bow.

Whitefield left April 2 bound for Pennsylvania and further evangelical work and orphanages. John Milledge had gone back to his logging work while he waited. But once he heard that Whitefield's sloop was down the river and past Tybee Island, he returned to Savannah.

With no attempt at concealment, in broad daylight and cheered by his neighbors, he brought Richard and Frances home. There were enough of Whitefield's disciples in the colony to pass on the word. Whitefield wrote time after time to protest the action, call it illegal and demand that the children be sent to the orphanage.

He never received a satisfactory answer. Richard and Frances remained at home until they were full-grown and ready to marry and care for themselves. John Milledge flourished as he reached maturity. He became a leading man in the colony.

His first official capacity was tithing man. Then he became quartermaster in the militia, in command of six men at Fort Argyle. He was afterwards captain of a company of rangers, a deft and canny frontier fighter. When the colony expanded, he turned plantation-owner, and was well-to-do, a vestryman and church-warden for Christ Church Parish and member of the Commons House of Assembly. He died in 1781, in the middle of the Revolutionary War.

But this account would not be complete if it failed to give mention of John Milledge's son. His name was also John, and he followed very closely in the tradition his father had established. With the outbreak of the Revolution, when he was eighteen, he was one of the six Liberty Boys in Savannah. He and the rest decided on the night of May 11, 1775 that they were going to raid the local British powder magazine.

They made the raid right under the muskets and bayonets of the British garrison troops, miraculously escaped with the powder. A good part of that they managed to put aboard a vessel bound for Boston, as assistance for the patriots there. Then they agreed that it would be sensible to leave Savannah. James Wright, the Royal Governor, had just put a price on John Milledge's head, and on that of his close companion, James Jackson.

Milledge and Jackson retaliated before they left. They abducted the governor, and tried to catch the Chief Justice, Stokes, in the same way. Stokes got out of the colony in self-defense, and Milledge and Jackson realized that their time had come, and released the governor.

They slipped across the Savannah River at night in a pirogue and went over to South Carolina. But when they met Revolutionary Army troops under General Moultrie out in the flatlands they were told they were British spies. Both of them were too well-dressed, and were known to come from prosperous plantation families. So they must be Loyalists and hiding their true feelings.

Milledge and Jackson told the Moultrie troops in pungent terms how wrong that reasoning was. But they were sentenced to death and about to be hanged when Moultrie had the good sense to send an officer in civilian clothing into Savannah to investigate the facts. The officer returned with the story of the powder, the Royal Governor and the Chief Justice. Ropes were taken away, and apologies expressed. John Milledge finished out the war in the Revolutionary Army. He was later governor in his own right, governor of the State of Georgia.

Bibliography

Adams, James Truslow, "The Founding of New England," Little, Brown and Company, Boston, Mass., 1939.

Andrews, Charles M., "The Colonial Period of American History," in four volumes, Yale University Press, New Haven, 1934.

Andrews, Matthew Page, "Virginia," Doubleday, Doran and Company, New York, 1937.

Betjeman, John, "An Oxford University Chest," John Miles, London, England, 1938.

Briant, Keith, "Oxford Limited," Farrar, Rinehart and Company, New York, 1938.

Coffin, Robert P. Tristram, "Kennebec, Cradle of America," Farrar and Rinehart Company, New York, 1937.

"Collections and Proceedings of the Maine Historical Society," Series 1, vol. 1, p. 302; Series 1, vol. 3, pp. 314, 355, 356, 358, 362, 373, 377, 381, 399, 402, 409, 413, 420, 433–34; Series 1, vol. 5, 370n., vol. 6, p. 191.

Collins, Henry Hill, "Complete Field Guide to American Wildlife," Harper and Brothers, New York, 1959.

Coulter, Ellis Merton, and Livengood, W. W., editors of "History of Georgia," American Book Company, New York, 1954.

Davis, William T., editor of "Bradford's History of Plymouth Plantation," Charles Scribner's Sons, New York, 1908.

Earle, Alice Morse, editor of "Diary of Anna Green Winslow," Houghton, Mifflin Company, Boston, 1894.

——, "Child Life in Colonial Days," The Macmillan Company, New York, 1899.

Halsey, Carolyn Du Little, "The Indians of Long Island," Hampton Press, West Hampton, New York, 1951.

Hart, Albert Bushnell, editor of "Commonwealth History of Massachusetts," in five volumes, New York State Historical Company, 1927–28.

Hill, Ralph Nading, "Yankee Kingdom," Harper and Brothers, New York, 1960.

Howe, George, "Mount Hope," The Viking Press, New York, 1959.

Howe, Henry F., "Salt Rivers of the Massachusetts Shore," Rinehart and Company, 1951.

Koskinen, Mildred Smith, article, "Pocahontas," in "A Cavalcade of Young Americans," edited by Carl Carmer, Lothrop, Lee and Shepherd Company, New York, 1958.

Lang, Andrew, "Oxford," J. B. Lippincott, Philadelphia, Pa., 1914.

Long Island Forum, article, "John Lyon Gardiner," Part II, July, 1960.

Morison, Samuel Eliot, "The Intellectual Life of New England," New York University Press, New York, 1956.

——, editor of "The Parkman Reader," Little, Brown and Company, Boston, 1955.

Morris, Richard B., editor of "Encyclopedia of American History," Harper and Brothers, New York, 1953.

Mowrer, Lillian T., "The Indomitable John Scott," Farrar, Straus and Cudahy, New York, 1960.

Payne, Robert, "The Island," Harcourt, Brace and Company, New York, 1958.

Phillips, James Duncan, "Salem in the Seventeenth Century," Houghton, Mifflin Company, Boston, 1933.

Phillips, Paul Chrisler, "The Fur Trade," in two volumes, University of Oklahoma Press, Norman, Oklahoma, 1961.

Platt, Rutherford, "Wilderness," Dodd, Mead and Company, New York, 1961.

Roberts, Kenneth, "Northwest Passage," Doubleday and Company, Garden City, New York, 1936.

Rowse, A. L., "The Elizabethans and America," Harper and Brothers, New York, 1959.

Sawtelle, William Otis, "Maine's Historic Trails and Waterways," Maine Development Commission, Augusta, Maine, 1932.

Semmes, Raphael, "Captains and Mariners of Early Maryland," Johns Hopkins Press, Baltimore, Maryland, 1937.

Strong, Reverend Titus, D.D., "The Deerfield Captive," A. Phelps and F. G. Tilton, Greenfield, Mass., 1884.

Tebbell, John, editor of "The Battle for North America," from the works of Francis Parkman, Doubleday and Company, Garden City, 1948.

Temple, Sarah B. Gober, and Coleman, Kenneth, "Georgia Journeys," University of Georgia Press, Athens, Georgia, 1961.

Wedgwood, C. V., "The King's Peace," The Macmillan Company, New York, 1955.

INDEX

THE AUTHOR

ROBERT CARSE and his wife make their home on Shelter Island, just off East Hampton, Long Island, and not far from Gardiner's Island and the home of David Gardiner and his family. He has been interested in the area and its history for years, and it was his research into the life of the Gardiners that led to his interest in other young colonials, and the writing of this book.

Mr. Carse is the author of six novels for young people, including *Winter of the Whale, Friends of the Wolf, The Winner* and *Great Venture.* He is also well known for his adult works—*Rum Row, Great Circle, The Age of Piracy, Deep Six*—and nine other works of fiction and nonfiction, as well as many stories and articles for both adults and young people.

As much a seaman as he is an author, Robert Carse has spent an equal amount of time on the water as off during the last forty years. He has sailed as an able sailor, gunner, master-at-arms, deck watch, and for ten years, chief mate. During World War II, he was a member of the ill-fated Murmansk Convoy which lost more than half of its ships in the famous 1942 run. He wrote of this experience in his book *There Go the Ships.* His latest adult work, *The Moonrakers,* is the story of the American clipper ships, which gave this country supremacy in the merchant trade.